CREATING JAZZ COUNTERPOINT

CREATING JAZZ COUNTERPOINT

New Orleans, Barbershop Harmony, and the Blues

Vic Hobson

UNIVERSITY PRESS OF MISSISSIPPI

JACKSON

www.upress.state.ms.us

Designed by Peter D. Halverson

The University Press of Mississippi is a member of the Association of American University Presses.

First printing 2014

∞

Library of Congress Cataloging-in-Publication Data

Hobson, Vic.
Creating jazz counterpoint : New Orleans, barbershop harmony, and the blues / Vic Hobson.
pages cm. — (American made music series)
Includes bibliographical references and index.
ISBN 978-1-61703-991-1 (cloth : alk. paper) — ISBN 978-1-61703-992-8 (ebook) 1. Jazz—Louisiana—New Orleans—History and criticism. 2. Blues (Music)—Louisiana—New Orleans—History and criticism. I. Title.
ML3508.8.N48H63 2014
781.65'3—dc23   2013033566
British Library Cataloging-in-Publication Data available

This book is dedicated to the memory of my father, Ronald Victor Hobson.
His Louis Armstrong record collection certainly started something.

CONTENTS

FOREWORD

THE QUESTIONS RAISED IN THIS BOOK BEGAN TO TAKE SHAPE AT A joint conference of the Historic Brass Society and the Institute of Jazz Studies at Rutgers University in 2005. I had written a paper for the conference questioning how the blues had become a part of New Orleans jazz.[1] Bruce Raeburn (curator of the Hogan Jazz Archive, New Orleans) suggested that the interviews that the archive held with early New Orleans jazzmen might be a good way forward. The following spring, as New Orleans struggled to recover from Hurricane Katrina, I took my first visit to the Crescent City. On my way back to England, I stopped off in New York and met briefly with Lewis Porter. Together we agreed that I should write an essay for *Jazz Perspectives*; the result was "New Orleans Jazz and the Blues," which appeared in the spring of 2011.[2] This was an historical essay that relied substantially on what early jazzmen of New Orleans said about their experiences of the blues. Despite the limited scope of the essay, it did establish that the blues—in all its forms—was known and performed by the early jazz bands of New Orleans. The question left unanswered was how these musicians had come to know the blues. This book explores this question.

The Hogan Jazz Archive has played a particularly important role in the writing of this book. Bruce Raeburn provided unprecedented access to the collections and valuable guidance. My visits to the archive also put me in contact with Lynn Abbott, whose encyclopedic knowledge of early blues and enthusiasm for the subject is an inspiration. Lynn asked me to write an essay for the *Jazz Archivist*. This gave me an opportunity to explore in some detail "Buddy Bolden's Blues."[3] He read earlier drafts, and his guidance, particularly in relation to quartet practices, has been essential. It was though Lynn that I approached David Evans and Craig Gill to get this book published. It is a privilege to have such knowledgeable advisors.

I was fortunate to receive a Woest Fellowship to the Historic New Orleans Collection to research the Papers of Frederic Ramsey Jr. This gave me access to the research notes and materials collected by both Fred Ramsey and Bill Russell. This became central to writing this book. My thanks to Alfred Lemmon, Mark Cave, Daniel Hammer, Siva Blake, Eric Seiferth, and Jennifer Navarra for their help in guiding me through these collections.

Financial support from the Arts and Humanities Research Council (AHRC) and Roberts Funding enabled me to travel extensively to conduct my research. It was through the AHRC and the support of Jonathan Impett (University of East Anglia) that I was awarded a Kluge Scholarship in 2007. I am very grateful to Carolyn T. Brown, Mary Lou Reker, and the staff and scholars at the Kluge Center of the Library of Congress for making this period so rewarding. I am especially indebted to Todd Harvey for guiding me through the Alan Lomax collection and to Michael Taft and Jennifer Cutting of the American Folklife Center.

Thanks too to Karl Koenig for access to his own archive material, his hospitality, and his introduction into the mysteries of baseball. Particularly important were the scrapbooks of R. Emmet Kennedy. By the time I appreciated the significance of Kennedy's folklore collections, the original scrapbooks had been split up between surviving family members. Karl Koenig had a copy of the complete collection.

There are, of course, many people who have played a part in advising, encouraging, and supplying me with material in the course of writing this book. I am sure that this is not an exhaustive list, and my apologies to anyone that I have unintentionally omitted. My thanks to Lawrence Gushee (University of Illinois); Joseph B. Borel (Gretna Historical Society); Greg Johnson (curator of the Mississippi Blues Archive); Paul Garon (Beasley Books); Pat Schroeder (Ursinus College); Azusa Nishimoto (Aoyama Gakuin University); Michael P. Bibler (University of Mary Washington); Minnie Handy Hanson (Handy Brothers); Gunther Schuller (Historic Brass Society); Trevor Herbert (Open University); David Sager (Library of Congress); Krin Gabbard (Stony Brook University); John J. Joyce (Tulane University); David Nathan, Graham Langley, and Chris Hodgkins (National Jazz Archive); Sharon Choa and Simon Waters (University of East Anglia); Jeff Nussbaum and Howard Weiner (Historic Brass Society); Gerhard Kubik (University of Vienna); Dennis Moore (Southern American Studies Association); John Howland and Steven F. Pond (*Jazz Perspectives*); and Neil Lerner (*American Music*).

CREATING JAZZ COUNTERPOINT

1

JAZZMEN

TODAY JAZZ IS STUDIED IN UNIVERSITIES, DISCUSSED AT ACADEMIC conferences, and is the subject of musicological research. It was not always so. Early jazz researchers were not, in the main, historians or musicologists, but enthusiasts—people for whom day jobs got in the way of their real passion—collecting "hot jazz." This was a small, dedicated band of phonograph record collectors in search of what were known at the time as "race recordings." At the center of the American section of the loose confederation of hot jazz collectors was Frederic Ramsey Jr.[1] After graduating from Princeton in 1936, Ramsey took a job in the production office with publishers Harcourt Brace. Given his interest in jazz, when a manuscript on jazz arrived at the office, he was asked to review it. As he would later recall, "I read it carefully and wrote an editor's report. The manuscript was miserable. . . . Out of 'sheer modesty,' I wrote in the last line 'I could make a better book on jazz.'"[2] The result was a landmark in jazz publishing, *Jazzmen* (1939).[3]

The appearance of *Jazzmen* was timely. Jazz had been a part of mainstream American culture for more than two decades, and by the middle of the thirties was enjoying unparalleled widespread acceptance. When *Jazzmen* appeared in 1939, it was the first book of its kind: it presented jazz as music with a history and firmly placed New Orleans at the origin.

Despite wartime restrictions, a U.S. Army and Navy edition for circulation among service personnel overseas appeared in 1945. After the war, overseas editions began to appear. The French edition in 1947 was "the first American book on jazz translated into a foreign language."[4] Sedgwick and Jackson produced an edition to satisfy the demands of the New Orleans revivalists in Britain in 1958; back in the States, Harcourt-Brace were preparing a "Giant Edition" for inclusion in their Harvest Book Series.

In retrospect, *Jazzmen*'s strength was also its weakness: it relied heavily on oral testimony of the jazzmen themselves. Because it had been published within a very short period and with a severely limited budget, there was very little time or opportunity to check the information for accuracy. The greatest weakness, many would argue, was that it relied heavily on the recollections of the cornet player Bunk Johnson. Johnson had been located working on a rice farm in New Iberia and claimed to have firsthand knowledge of the early years of jazz. As Johnson increasingly became promoted as a figurehead of the traditional jazz revival, he and his testimony came under scrutiny. Historically, much that he said simply did not seem credible. He claimed he and Buddy Bolden had started jazz in New Orleans. But there was just a single photograph of Bolden and his band, and Johnson was not in the photograph. Even if he had been in the Bolden band, there was nothing that proved Bolden had any significant role in the making of early jazz. Critics would also come to question when Johnson was born. Even by his own testimony he was still in short pants when Bolden was musically active.

A second weakness that is perhaps less obvious is that *Jazzmen* did not identify its informants. Although a good number of interviews were conducted for the book, in most cases it is not possible to know who said what. As the credibility of Bunk Johnson became increasingly questioned, it was also assumed that much of the more doubtful information came from Bunk. This, it turns out, was by no means always the case. The only way to test this would have been to have access to the original interview notes, and a full set of these notes has only recently become publicly available.[5]

While *Jazzmen* was widely read and commented on, a book on New Orleans jazz by a Belgian lawyer, Robert Goffin, has received far less attention. Goffin visited New Orleans in 1944 and employed similar methods to the *Jazzmen* authors: he interviewed local jazzmen. Goffin's book, *La Nouvelle-Orléans Capital du Jazz*, appeared in 1946 and has never been published in English. A rough translation provides a fascinating insight into the development of New Orleans jazz. It would be a further decade before the Hogan Jazz Archive at Tulane University would begin collecting interviews with local jazz musicians. By this time, a number of musicians who had played with Bolden, and who Goffin interviewed, had already died.

Fred Ramsey died in 1995, and his personal archive was acquired by the Historic New Orleans Collection. In 2009, I was fortunate to receive a Woest Fellowship to the HNOC to research the papers of Ramsey. These papers included the interview notes from *Jazzmen*. This was informative because these notes show that some of the claims that have been attributed to Bunk Johnson did not originate with him, but rather with Willy Cornish, Bolden's trombonist.[6] It was Cornish who provided *Jazzmen* with the photograph of Bolden and his band. Cornish is in this photograph, and clearly had an unrivaled knowledge of the role Bolden played in the early years of jazz. Significantly, Cornish confirmed that Bunk Johnson had played with the Bolden band. This, in turn, fundamentally affects the credibility of Bunk Johnson's recollections regarding Bolden. This is not only of historical interest. Bunk Johnson made a considerable number of recordings recreating the music of the Bolden era. These recordings have been largely treated with skepticism by musicologists. In the knowledge that Johnson did play with Bolden, these recordings assume new significance.

Wilder Hobson (who contributed to *Jazzmen*) also published *American Jazz Music* in 1939. An issue he raised in the book is still unresolved: how did jazz counterpoint function? By the time New Orleans musicians began to record after World War I, a recognizable New Orleans style of jazz had developed. This was a largely improvised, polyphonic music, rooted in the tonality of the blues. However, as Wilder Hobson notes in *American Jazz Music*, the idea of jazz counterpoint "has often appalled academic musicians, who have said that it was impossible, or at least that the musical results would be impossible."[7] The question this raises is how could a group of musicians apparently improvise simultaneously and produce music of consistent harmonic and melodic relations? Retrospectively, as many revival recordings testify, it is quite possible to reproduce New Orleans style jazz, but it is quite another thing to do this with a novel repertoire. We can, of course, using conventional music theory analyze *what* New Orleans jazz musicians played. What we have been unable to do (so far) is to describe *why* they played as they did. Given the significance of jazz in the music making of the twentieth century, this is of some importance.

Central to the argument made in this book is that jazz counterpoint is the application of the principles of African American four-part singing (commonly called barbershop) to the instrumentation of a jazz band. The historical case for the African American origins of barbershop harmony has already been established by Lynn Abbott in his groundbreaking essay "Play That Barber Shop Chord."[8] Abbott's paper is essentially historical rather than musicological. It has long been recognized that the tonality of the blues is an essential element in jazz. This book expands on Abbott's research to show how barbershop quartet practices relate to the tonality of the blues and how this, in turn, relates to the polyphony of New Orleans jazz. Critical to this argument is an understanding of barbershop cadences. Sigmund Spaeth produced two books on *Barber Shop Ballads*, the first in 1925 and a revised edition in 1940.[9] Both books provide extensive analysis of barbershop cadences and the vocal practices that underpinned them. He did not, however, provide any harmonic analysis in terms of chord symbols. I have added these to enable comparison with sheet music and transcriptions.

An understanding of the nature and principles that underpin New Orleans jazz also makes it possible to engage with some of the outstanding issues in early jazz. Was New Orleans the unique birthplace of jazz? Was New Orleans style only played in New Orleans? Did the same musical practices develop among African Americans, Creoles, and white New Orleans musicians, and what light does this shed on the racial origins of jazz? It may never be possible to answer these questions with certainty, but an understanding of how and why New Orleans jazz counterpoint developed may make it possible to form a reasoned judgment and suggest further lines of investigation.

2

THE BOLDEN LEGEND

THE LEGEND OF BUDDY BOLDEN DID NOT BEGIN WITH THE PUBLICA-
tion of *Jazzmen*. In 1933, African American journalist E. Belfield Spriggins
first described the role that Bolden played in the early years of jazz. Donald
Marquis in 1971 discovered back copies of these articles in the *Louisiana
Weekly*. A search of the telephone directories established that Spriggins was
still alive. Unfortunately, in 1965 Hurricane Betsy had destroyed Spriggins's
personal archive, and the experience of losing his life's work had rendered
him speechless. He never did recover and died in 1973.[1]

In 1933, Spriggins wrote: "For quite some years now there has been an
unusual amount of discussion concerning the popular form of music popu-
larly called 'jazz.' The name followed the old name 'rag time' which was a
more or less modified form of jazz. Seemingly, New Orleans has been either
too modest to enter the discussion or entirely disinterested in the matter."[2]
Today we assume that New Orleans had a particular and significant role
in the early years of jazz. However, when jazz became a national craze the
New Orleans Times-Picayune of June 20, 1918, stated the position of the
paper. Since it had been suggested, "this particular form of musical vice had
its birth in this city, . . . we do not recognize the honor of parenthood, but
with such a story in circulation, it behooves us to be the last to accept the
atrocity in polite society."[3] Spriggins's articles made clear that, more than a
decade later, New Orleans polite society had little interest in exploring the
question further.

These articles contain the first known reference to Buddy Bolden as an
important figure in the early years of jazz. Spriggins interviewed Willy Cornish, Bolden's trombone player, who told him about Bolden.

> Many years ago jazz tunes in their original form were heard in the
> Crescent City. Probably one of the earliest heard was one played by
> King Bolden's Band. It seems that one night while playing at Odd

Fellows Hall, Perdido near Rampart St., it became very hot and stuffy in the place and a discussion arose among the members of Bolden's band about the foul air. The next day William Cornish, the trombonist with the band, composed a "tune" to be played by the band. The real words are unprintable but these will answer.

"Thought I heard old Bolden say
Rotten gut Rotten gut!
Take it away."

The rendition of this number became an overnight sensation and the reputation of Bolden's band became a household word with the patrons of the Odd Fellows Hall, Lincoln and Johnson Parks, and several other popular dance halls around the city.[4]

When six years later the *Jazzmen* authors began their work, Charles Edward Smith also located Cornish living at 2024 Perdido Street. Cornish gave his date of birth as August 1, 1874. He told Smith that he was the only member of Bolden's "original" band still alive.[5]

Cornish had a photograph of Bolden and his band that included Cornish in the lineup. For nearly seventy years the photograph that he loaned to Charles Edward Smith (it was not returned, and the whereabouts of the original is unknown) has intrigued jazz scholars. Which way around should it be? As printed in *Jazzmen* it appeared with Jimmy Johnson (the bass player) on the left.[6] This did not appear to be correct; in a New Orleans band, the bass player is traditionally on the right. Al Rose and Edmond Souchon in *New Orleans Jazz: A Family Album* decided to reverse the image to correct this apparent mistake.[7] The paradox now was that Johnson, on bass, and the guitarist, Brock Mumford, were playing left-handed. That did not seem correct either; they were not left-handed players. Alden Ashford cleared up some of the mystery through reasoning that clarinets are not made symmetrically. Looked at from the front, the keys depressed by the player's little fingers appear on different sides and at different heights. This is not reversible. Despite the poor quality of the image, the photograph, as it first appeared in *Jazzmen*, was a reversed image. Rose and Souchon were correct and Johnson on bass should have been on the right. It therefore followed that Johnson and Mumford were posing left-handed for some inexplicable reason.[8] Charles Edward Smith's interview notes from his interview with Willy Cornish suggest a reason for this. Cornish had shown Smith the

Figure 1: Tintype photograph of a guitarist circa 1890s

photograph and identified the members of the band: "The photo line-up: left to right. Jimmy Johnson, bass; Bubby Bolden [sic], cornet; Jeff Mumford, guitar (sitting); Willy Cornish, key trombone; Frank Lewis, b clarinet, sitting; Willy Warner, C clarinet, standing."[9]

Evidently, the photograph, as it first appeared in *Jazzmen*, was as it was when Cornish first showed it to Charles Edward Smith, with Johnson on the left. It follows that since this was a reverse image, the photographic process itself was responsible for the reversal. The most likely explanation is that the Bolden band photograph was a "tintype":[10] a photograph made directly onto a plate of metal (not actually tin), coated with a layer of light sensitive chemicals. In this process, there is no negative and the image appears reversed. An example of this process is a well-known tintype of Billy the Kid.[11] For some years, historians questioned whether Billy the Kid was left-handed because a photograph showed him with his gun on his left side. The picture, we now know, was a tintype.

It seems everybody was correct. The photograph, as it appeared in *Jazzmen*, was as Willy Cornish had shown it to Smith; this was a reverse image produced by the tintype process. Rose and Souchon were therefore right, from the perspective of what the photographer saw, to reverse the image and put Jimmy Johnson on the right; this corrected the anomalies that Ashforth had noticed with regard to the clarinets. What this does not explain is why Johnson and Mumford posed left-handed. A likely explanation is that this was a trick of the trade. An experienced tintype photographer would know that the image would be reversed. There is strong evidence to show that to "correct" this reversal of image, a practice had developed to pose string players left-handed. Figure 1 is a tintype of a guitarist taken sometime in the 1890s.[12] The thicker bass strings (that should be on the top) are on the bottom. This is because the guitarist flipped the guitar over and posed left-handed; the "tintype" would therefore show him as a right-handed guitar player.

Because Willy Cornish was the only surviving member of Bolden's original band, he was the only informant that the *Jazzmen* authors could depend upon for accurate information about Bolden. Charles Edward Smith produced a report of their interview that ran to little more than three pages of typewritten notes. Smith had planned to do a follow-up interview to find out more. When he called for a second interview Cornish was not home; he was not in good health and died in January 1942. This was the only opportunity that the *Jazzmen* authors would get to hear firsthand information about Bolden's original band from someone who had definitely played with Bolden. Consequently, the *Jazzmen* authors were required to get further corroboration from sources that were perhaps less reliable.

Jazzmen claims that Bolden had been a barber. Many New Orleans musicians were barbers, and barber shops were meeting places for musicians looking for work. In an age when there were few telephones, the barber shop provided a way for musicians and promoters to keep in contact. What *Jazzmen* did not make clear was that the story that Bolden was a barber came from Preston Jackson. According to Jackson, Bolden "had a barber shop on Franklin and Perdido St; played at Tintype Hall, Liberty and Franklin. Tintype Hall is a place where all the 'hustlers' would be laid out when they were killed, gamblers, hard working musicians, etc."[13] There is nothing to substantiate either that Bolden was a barber, or that there was ever a venue called Tintype Hall. This is not surprising given that Jackson was born around 1903, and had no firsthand knowledge of Buddy Bolden and his band.[14]

Louis Jones was a drinking companion of Buddy Bolden and was a barber. When he moved to New Orleans in 1894 they were "like young men, bumin' [sic] together" and they would "drink and have fun with women."

Jones opened a New Orleans barber shop in 1899. He said that Bolden began playing "three or four years" before that.[15] Jones remembered, "Buddy Bolden learned how to play cornet under Manuel Hall."[16] He also said, "Bolden could read music . . . because he'd studied with this professor."[17] Because Hall did not move to New Orleans until September 1894, this suggests that 1895 is the earliest date for Bolden to begin his musical education and subsequent playing career.[18] Jones was adamant that Bolden was not a barber. "Buddy Bolden ain't never had no barber shop. . . . He never worked in no barber shop. . . . He used to bum wid [sic] barbers, but he never worked in a barber shop."[19] It seems likely that Bolden's association with Jones may explain why this story circulated.[20]

Another story that the *Jazzmen* authors heard was that Bolden "ran the *Cricket*, a local newspaper. 'Spider' would take him all the scandal and he would publish it."[21] Jones was adamant: "No, he had nothin' to do with no Cricket. . . . 'Cause Bolden didn't bother with 'The Cricket,' 'cause 'The Cricket' was in everybody's business . . . and if he fooled with—if he—Buddy fooled with 'The Cricket,' they'd meddle in his business."[22]

Interestingly, a number of editions of the *Cricket* survive. Lamar Middleton, the editor and publisher, set out the paper's ambitions in the first issue in March 1896: "It is proposed to establish in New Orleans a fortnightly paper which shall chronicle and discuss matters of current interest in society, light literature, music and the theaters; and shall furnish a medium of expression to local literary talent." In the *Cricket* "politics will be of decidedly minor importance; and idle gossip of a social or other nature will be absolutely avoided."[23] An ad in the July 1897 issue may have some relevance to the Bolden story: "The Marechal Neil String Band will furnish music for balls, picnics, parties or excursions, at very reasonable rates. Address either of the following gentlemen: Mr. Mamday, leader, Polambo's saloon (Carrolton [sic]); W. Warner, 2017 First St; W. Lewis, 5215 Annunciation St; H. Young, 5133 Annunciation St; E. Bazile 1027 Austerlitz St; L. M. Little, General Manager, 5517 Coliseum St."[24]

Was "W. Warner" Willy Warner the clarinetist in Bolden's band, and who is "W. Lewis"? Could this just be a typographical error and a reference to Frank Lewis, Bolden's other clarinetist? Searches of Soards' City Directory of 1897 provide nothing conclusive. Another possible reason for Bolden's association with the *Cricket* emerged in an interview with Bunk Johnson. He claimed: "Buddy inspired a few slanderous articles. Actually, it was Otis Watts, a friend of Buddy, who wrote the *Cricket*."[25] It is unfortunate that only four editions of this paper survive. If the paper did carry these advertisements, and articles by Otis Watts on a regular basis, they could potentially throw considerable light on New Orleans's music scene at the time.[26]

Another legend that has persisted is that Bolden played for the last time on Labor Day 1906. The New Orleans piano player Richard M. Jones (b. 1892) told the *Jazzmen* authors, "Buddy Bolden 'fell out' on a Labor Day parade." He "went on a rampage," was "too excited," and "played himself out, played too hard." According to Jones, he "was taken to the asylum soon after."[27] When *Jazzmen* was first published, this appears to have been the only source of the story. It is not in dispute that Bolden became mentally unstable by this time. There are two press reports of Bolden attacking his mother with a water pitcher in March 1906.[28] It is also a matter of record that he was committed to Jackson Asylum in June 1907. However, it is doubtful that Bolden "fell out" in the 1906 Labor Day parade. It is likely that this legend conflates two stories: Bolden's mental problems and the death of William Spillis. The *Times-Picayune* of September 4, 1906, carried the following story, under the title "Died in Parade: A Colored Musician Succumbs to the Heat": "About 11 o'clock yesterday forenoon as the colored labor parade was passing along Washington Avenue, between Dryades and Rampart Streets, William Spillis, a colored musician, a member of the band heading the Teamsters and Loaders' Union, fell from heat exhaustion in the middle of the street. The ambulance was summoned, but before it reached the scene Spillis was dead."[29]

A question that has intrigued researchers is whether Bolden made a cylinder recording. On this question Louis Jones was less helpful: "I don't know, I don't know . . . Maybe they did, and maybe I didn't know it." The significance of this is that the white Original Dixieland Jazz Band claimed they were the "creators of jazz," and they made the first jazz record. If Bolden had indeed recorded, and if this recording survived, then this would be highly significant. According to Willy Cornish, the recording session took place sometime between 1890 and 1898; it was probably a march rather than a blues or a "stomp"; this, Smith reasoned, was because it was made for a "white record company." The record, Cornish told him, was "to please a white friend . . . whose family ran a grocery and butcher shop in New Orleans."[30]

The common bond that united the *Jazzmen* authors was that they were record collectors—college educated young men who had come to know jazz through the "race" recordings of the 1920s. What united the *Jazzmen* authors would also divide them; the Bolden cylinder was too great a prize.

Accordingly, Charles Edward Smith omitted any mention of the Bolden cylinder in his report to the other writers. However, he did decide to let Bill Russell and Steve Smith in on the secret. On April 16, 1939, Smith wrote to Russell: "I told Cornish I'd pay at least ten bucks for the record, also asked him to keep it secret. . . . I also said that if the record were re-recorded through me that we would see he got a little royalty on each copy sold." Charles Edward Smith, Bill Russell, and Steve Smith were members of the Hot Record Society. The plan was to keep the Bolden cylinder secret from Frederic Ramsey and the others. The intention was to find the cylinder and issue it through the society. The problem, as Charles Edward Smith realized, was that the record would probably be in the public domain. Accordingly, he wrote, "I imagine the Hot Record Society could protect itself by a little introductory speech at the beginning of the record, enabling us to copyright the master and thus give Cornish a little royalty (whatever is regular)."[31] This would, of course, be extremely profitable and great publicity for the book launch. The plan failed; they did not find the cylinder.

As Smith was about to leave after having interviewed Cornish in 1939, he asked, "You're sure about that cylinder, aren't you?" Cornish replied that he was, and that "he'd heard it many times." He then told Smith, "I knew a man had a copy . . . his brother or some member of the family might have one." He gave Smith the name of a German-American shopkeeper. Smith found a number in the phone book and succeed in tracing down the family, only to discover that a number of old cylinder recordings went to the dump a few years earlier. Smith was convinced that the Bolden cylinder was among these. Undeterred, even as the galley proofs of the book were being prepared in July 1939, he still wanted to keep knowledge of the Bolden cylinder restricted to the Historic Record Society. On July 14, he wrote to Bill Russell. "I have not heard from Cornish. He probably is too ill to get a letter out. However, I will ask [Leonard] Bechet if he has time to see Cornish. That way we might get a lead. My guess is the record may have sold in the south only. I believe we will find it eventually, and it will be worthwhile to keep the search as quiet as possible."[32]

Smith still did not reveal the name of Oscar Zahn (the grocer who was thought to have had a copy of the Bolden cylinder) even in 1954 when he retold this story in *Saturday Review*. In the same year, Fred Ramsey had interviewed Edmund Wise as part of his research into Buddy Bolden. Wise told him that in 1924, he had visited Bolden in East Louisiana State Mental Hospital, and Bolden wanted to know "about a white fellow who had a bar" named Oscar Zahn. It seems that Bolden was not interested in the health of his mother and sister; his main concern was this white bar owner. A year later Fred Ramsey met up with Tom Bethel and relayed this information to him. Bethel blurted out: "But that's amazing! That's the guy—that's the man who did the recording! Oscar Zahn! I believe they also called him 'Dutchie.' That's the one Charles Edward Smith tried to reach—perhaps he did. And you didn't know that?"[33] It was more than thirty-five years since *Jazzmen* had been published and this was the first time that Fred Ramsey knew the name of the man Willy Cornish said had a copy of the cylinder.

Whether there was a cylinder recording of the Bolden Band will probably never be known. For one thing, if a cylinder was found it would be virtually impossible to verify. It was not, according to Cornish, the first jazz recording, and it is unlikely that it could be distinguished from other recordings of the period. According to Cornish, it was made privately, and it probably would not have had the name of Bolden or his band marked on it. Only through provenance could the recording be reliably identified. Given that the Zahn family disposed of their cylinder recordings, it would be difficult to connect any cylinder found back to Bolden. None of this, however, argues against the possibility that the cylinder was made. When Cornish told Smith of the recording, he can have had little idea of the value that Smith and later researchers would place on it. Cornish provided the name of a man who had a copy of the recording and said he had heard it many times. He provided the most reliable firsthand evidence we have of Bolden and his band. It therefore seems reasonable to give Willy Cornish the benefit of the doubt. His other recollections of Bolden (with the exception of his dating of events) have been corroborated by later research. There is no reason to think Cornish less reliable in relation to the cylinder.

Despite the best efforts of the *Jazzmen* authors and others, firm evidence of the existence of Buddy Bolden remained elusive in the following decades. In 1958 the Hogan Jazz Archive in New Orleans began collecting oral history interviews with surviving New Orleans jazz musicians. Of those interviewed, around 200 were born before 1900; consequently, they may have had some knowledge of Bolden and his band. Consistently those interviewed said that Bolden was famous, that he played loud, and that he went insane. What was absent was any fresh evidence to support the Bolden myth. As late as 1963, the *Melody Maker* carried the story "I Thought I Heard Buddy Bolden Say: But How Could You If He Never Lived?" In the article, Brian Woolly argued:

I've always smelled a rat in this Bolden fable. . . . Nobody has ever produced tangible proof that this "popular idol" of New Orleans jazz ever
lived, let alone blew red hot cornet. For instance, Louis Armstrong
has repeatedly glossed over Bolden's existence in his books. There are
no records. You can largely discount all of Jelly Roll Morton's roman-
tic ramblings at the American Library of Congress because he was
going along with the myth. It's a storyline dreamed up by somebody.
Nobody has yet proved that Buddy Bolden lived. The fact is that jazz
as we know it today was started by the Original Dixieland Jass Band—
and no one else.[34]

New evidence of the existence of Buddy Bolden did not emerge until
February 1974. Diana Rose, the wife of the jazz historian Al Rose, found an
old letter in the French Market in New Orleans. The letter was an invitation
to a 1903 Mardi Gras Ball at the "Ladies Providence Hall" where the music
would be provided by "Prof. Bolden's Orchestra."[35]

The hunt for Buddy Bolden was now on. A few months later in June 1974,
Fred Ramsey wrote to his publisher (Oxford University Press) to say that
he had secured a "senior fellowship" from the National Endowment for the
Humanities (and a verbal commitment from the Ford Foundation) to write
a book on Bolden, and asking if the OUP would be interested in publishing
it.[36] They were.

Fred Ramsey and his wife, Amelia, visited New Orleans in 1974 and again
in 1975. They said that they had "dug out a mass of material" which was
more than they dared anticipate. This included more that 300 interview
transcripts and a collection of some 5,000 photocopies of "pertinent documents." They had uncovered birth and death certificates, "journals, newspa-
pers, music," and had interviewed "about two dozen" people. This workload
necessitated that their projected delivery date for the manuscript would be
the spring of 1977. Ramsey also pointed out, in his letter to Oxford University Press, that "Amelia's collaboration has been total"; therefore "she must
share the byline on the publication."[37]

By the end of 1977, the Oxford University Press was enquiring if Ramsey
knew of a book by Donald M. Marquis, *In Search of Buddy Bolden: First
Man of Jazz*. Ramsey had seen a number of extracts of Marquis's unpublished book. He pointed out that "Marquis has little writing experience,"
and "no background in jazz studies." However, he grudgingly conceded that
Marquis's book might turn out a "fairly reliable source book of the kind
prepared by jazz afficionados [sic] to consult." More than thirty years later,

this book is still the most reliable source of information on Buddy Bolden. Ramsey's lack of progress on his own book, he explained, was due to Amelia's poor health and a leaky roof at home.[38] In January 1979 Amelia died. Sheldon Meyer, senior vice president of Oxford University Press, wrote to send his "deepest sympathy," and commented that a "fitting memorial to her would be the publication of the book."[39]

Frederic Ramsey Jr. died in 1995 with the book on Bolden unpublished. By 2006 the Historic New Orleans Collection had acquired Ramsey's personal papers, including his research material on Buddy Bolden. A survey of the material in the collection suggests that Ramsey only ever wrote an abstract—which he used to get the publishing contract—and a draft of the foreword to the book. Despite this, in a 1988 interview with Pete Whelan for *78 Quarterly*, Ramsey had said that there would be "an awful lot that will come out in this book that isn't in any other book or article about Bolden." Ramsey had provisionally titled his book *Buddy Bolden and His New Orleans*.

Central to Ramsey's argument about the emergence of jazz in New Orleans was the Robert Charles Riot of July 1900, when the shooting of a police officer triggered race riots in New Orleans. Responding to a report of "two suspicious looking negroes" that were sitting on a doorstep of 2815 Dryades Street, Sergeant Jules C. Aucoin and two other officers of the New Orleans Police Department went to investigate. The police officers gave varying accounts of who fired first, but Robert Charles fled the scene, bleeding from a gunshot wound.[40] Four days later Charles was located, hiding at 1208 Saratoga. Before he was killed, he shot twenty-four white people including a further four police officers.[41] There were further casualties as race violence erupted throughout the city.

Ramsey argued that after the riot the older downtown "Creoles of Color" still "clung to old customs, old ways of doing things, and to a traditional music of the dance and concert hall. They went to and played in the opera, and maintained exclusive dancing salons from which the uptown blacks were excluded"—whereas, according to Ramsey, the music of Bolden was "based on what had been an emerging sense of pride and identity. This sense had been squelched by the [Robert Charles] Riot, forced underground. Yet it was Bolden who grasped the sense, knew it was there, kept it alive. He played on this suppressed undertone of feeling, bringing into play a language, and a communication inexorably built into black consciousness."[42]

Ramsey only wrote this as a draft and perhaps he would have later revised his thoughts. There are a number of lines of argument that are unclear and open to question. While there were some older Creoles of Color who may well have clung to their previous customs, for many of a younger generation, including musicians, there was little choice other than to integrate with uptown African Americans. As the Creole violinist Paul Dominguez explained:

> See, us downtown people, we didn't think so much of this rough Uptown jazz until we couldn't make a living otherwise . . . they made a fiddler out of a violinist—me, I'm talking about. A fiddler is *not* a violinist, but a violinist can be a fiddler. If I wanted to make a living, I had to be rowdy like the other group. I had to jazz it or rag it or any other damn thing . . . Bolden caused all that. He caused these younger Creoles, men like Bechet and Keppard, to have a different style altogether from the old heads like Tio and Perez. I don't know how they do it. But goddamn, they'll do it. Can't tell you what's there on the paper, but just play the hell out of it.[43]

The extent to which jazz was forced underground by the Robert Charles Riot is also open to question. Robert Charles became something of a folk hero in black New Orleans, and consequently a song circulated that told of his deeds. But, as Jelly Roll Morton recalled, he found it best to forget that he knew the song "in order to get along with the world on the peaceful side."[44] While this particular song may have been forced underground, there is little to suggest that the Robert Charles Riot had a similar impact on the development of jazz more generally.

Fred Ramsey was not a musician, and when he was asked if he could describe what Bolden and his band might have sounded like, he said, "I wouldn't risk it. I don't know music well enough. I would be faking. What I concentrate on is getting descriptions of living musicians who had heard Bolden, and that's better than I can do."[45] Although *Buddy Bolden: First Man of Jazz* had been the provocative title of Donald Marquis's book, this title was largely a marketing strategy on the part of the publisher. In the 2005 reprint, Marquis explained, "My personal choice for the title was 'In search of the Bolden Legend.' As the name 'Bolden' was relatively unknown in 1978, an editorial decision was made to use 'Jazz' in the title." That Bolden was the first to play jazz was a claim "not made in the book."[46]

Whether Bolden was or was not the first man of jazz is not nearly as straightforward a question as it might first appear. It is not even known if jazz is uniquely of New Orleans origin. There is, however, wider agreement that there is a New Orleans style of jazz. New Orleans jazz has a number of distinct features. In New Orleans jazz the instruments have independent melodic lines that weave together to produce what has been called jazz counterpoint.[47] When academically trained musicians attempted to play New Orleans jazz they needed to use stock arrangements. These were generally produced from a piano score. This time-consuming process of making arrangements required the involvement of a skilled arranger to transfer the piano score into an orchestration. Many of the New Orleans bands used stock arrangements too. It was essential for dance bands to keep abreast of the latest tunes. However, some of the New Orleans musicians could do something else; they could *apparently* produce an arrangement in performance. Without the aid of musical notation, they could produce music with a number of musicians improvising at the same time. Quite how they did this is still not fully understood.

New Orleans jazz developed out of (or perhaps alongside) ragtime. The early published rags differed from later jazz in a number of ways. Ragtime tunes usually had a number of different strains. Some early jazz compositions retained the multi-strain form, but generally, there was a move toward simpler verse and chorus form in popular song. In improvised jazz performance this was often further simplified and only the chorus was played. It was much easier for improvising musicians to restrict their performance to a single repeated chorus, used as the basis for improvisation, rather than attempt to improvise on a complex multi-themed rag.

A second significant difference was instrumentation. A typical dance band arrangement for a ragtime band included first and second violin, viola, cello, bass, piccolo, cornet, clarinet, trombone, and drums. The string players led this ensemble; the brass and woodwind played supporting harmonic roles. By contrast, the cornet led a jazz band.

A third change that took place as ragtime gave way to jazz was rhythmic. In ragtime, there are two down beats in each measure; this is march-time or 2/4 time. The syncopation of ragtime results from accents to up-beats (or subdivisions of these). Corresponding with this two-beat music popular dances of the ragtime period were the one-step, the two-step, and the turkey trot. With the appearance of the blues, new four-beat music began to change dance styles. The fox trot, in particular, became synonymous with W. C. Handy's "The Memphis Blues" (1912).[48]

Another significant difference noticed by early commentators was a difference between the harmony of ragtime and jazz. In 1922 an article by Carl Engel, titled "Jazz: A Musical Discussion," appeared in *Atlantic Monthly*.

Between the earlier "rag" and the "blues," there was this distinction: the rag had been mainly a thing of rhythm, of syncopation; the blues were syncopation relished with spicier harmonies. In addition to these two elements of music, rhythm and harmony, the people—who in the beginning had known but one thing: melody fastened upon a primitive and weak harmonic structure of "Barbershop" chords—the people, I say, who had stepwise advanced from melody and rhythms to harmony, lastly discovered counterpoint. And the result of this last discovery is jazz. In other words, jazz is rag-time, plus "Blues," plus orchestral polyphony; it is the combination, in the popular music current, of melody, rhythm, harmony, and counterpoint.[49]

The new music of jazz had a new tonality. Jazz used harmonies that were different from ragtime compositions and that, according to this author, were rooted in barbershop harmony. Critically, these harmonic features were associated with the tonality of the blues.

"I Thought I Heard Buddy Bolden Say"

The tune that New Orleans musicians consistently associated with Buddy Bolden was known variously as "Funky Butt," "I Thought I Heard Buddy Bolden Say," or simply "Buddy Bolden's Blues." William Russell and Stephen Smith described this tune in *Jazzmen* as Buddy Bolden's "theme" song.[50] The song is important for this reason and also because two very similar tunes were published, one as a cakewalk ("The Cake Walk in the Sky") in 1899 and the other as a rag ("The St. Louis Tickle") in 1904.[51] "Buddy Bolden's Blues" therefore provides a specific example of how the music of Buddy Bolden may have related to the prevailing musical trends of the period, and presents an opportunity to compare the published rag and cakewalk with Morton's recording of "Buddy Bolden's Blues."

According to Morton, "Buddy Bolden's Blues," a song that he dates to 1902, "is the earliest blues that was the real thing. That is a variation from the real barrelhouse blues." He goes on to say:

The composer was Buddy Bolden, the most powerful trumpet player I've ever heard or ever was known. The name of this was named by some old honky-tonk people. While he played this, they sang a little theme to it. He was a favorite in New Orleans at the time.[52]

I thought I heard Buddy Bolden say,
Dirty nasty stinkin' butt, take it away,
A dirty nasty stinkin' butt, take it away,
Oh, Mister Bolden, play.

I thought I heard Bolden play,
Dirty nasty stinkin' butt, take it away,
A funky butt, stinky butt, take away,
And let Mister Bolden play. . . .

Later on this tune was, uh, I guess I'd have to say, stolen by some author I don't know anything about—I don't remember his name—and
published under the title of "St. Louis Tickler." But with all the proof in
the world, this tune was wrote by Buddy Bolden. Plenty old musicians
know it.[53]

The publication of "The St. Louis Tickle" in 1904 coincided with the
World's Fair in St. Louis. The composition, credited to Barney and Seymore,
used a tune similar to "Buddy Bolden's Blues" for the second strain of this
"Rag Time Two Step," and it is this strain that Morton believed had been
"stolen" from Buddy Bolden.[54]

"Barney & Seymore" is probably a pseudonym for Theron C. Bennett
(1879–1937), a Missouri pianist better known for purchasing W. C. Handy's
"The Memphis Blues" in 1912.[55] It is possible that Bennett employed a pre-
existing tune such as "Buddy Bolden's Blues" in his "St. Louis Tickle." It
could also be that he came to know the tune from another source. It is likely
that the tune was in general circulation along the Mississippi River.[56]

Roy Carew began work in Gretna in 1904 and later recalled a white office
boy at his place of work singing:

I thought I heard Miss Suzie shout,
Open up the windows and let the breeze blow out.[57]

Edmond Souchon recalled another version of the song from New Orleans.
When he was a child of four or five years old, around 1901 or 1902, his nanny
would sing:

Ain't that man got a funny walk [sic]
Doin' the 'Ping-Pong' 'round Southern park.

Nigger man, white man, take him away,
I thought I heard him say.[58]

A further version is associated with New Orleans trombonist, Jack Carey.

I Thought I Heard Jack Carey Say
Funky Butt, Funky Butt take it away![59]

The Composer Virgil Thomson remembered it as a river song heard in his boyhood in Kansas City, and Dr. Newman Ivey White reported it in his book *American Negro Folk-song* in the following form, sung as a work song by Negro laborers in Augusta, Georgia:

Thought I heard—huh!
Judge Pequette say—huh!
Forty-five dol-lars—huh!
Take him away—huh!

Dr. White adds his own memory of the tune as a street song in 1903 in Statesville, North Carolina.[60]

"Buddy Bolden's Blues" is a song, and songs may not have been typical of Bolden's dance repertoire. Beatrice Alcorn, who attended his dances around 1904, said that when Bolden played, "no one sang lyrics as they might have done at other dances."[61] On the other hand, it may be that Bolden adapted his repertoire for different venues. Because it is a song, we have the advantage of being able to see what, if anything, the lyrics tell us that would help in the dating of "Buddy Bolden's Blues."

If we review the lyrics of a version of "Buddy Bolden's Blues" as recorded by Morton in 1939, it included the lines:

I thought I heard Judge Fogarty say,
Thirty days in the market, take him away.
Give him a good broom to sweep with, take him away.
I thought I heard him say.[62]

The lyric is a reference to Judge John J. Fogarty, who was born in New Orleans in 1865, and became the presiding judge of the First Recorders Court in 1904. The *Behrman Administration Biography*, published in 1912, noted of Fogarty that "He and his fame have been celebrated in poetry and song and a certain popular ditty may be heard every day on Canal Street."[63] Judge Fogarty's grandson Joseph also recalled:

> I remember the song that was later recorded by Jelly Roll Morton. I can remember my father singing it. The way I always heard it—"I thought I heard Judge Fogarty say, '25 dollars or thirty days.'" My father also told me that when they had vaudeville shows at the Orpheum they were constantly cracking jokes about Judge Fogarty from the stage. And another thing, when people play poker in New Orleans, if they hold three tens, they call it "Judge Fogarty"—thirty days.[64]

The other reference that Morton makes in his recording that may help date the song is to the valve trombonist Frankie Duson, who took over the leadership of Buddy Bolden's band as Bolden's health deteriorated.[65]

> *Thought I heard Frankie Dusen shout,*
> *Gal, give me the money, I'm gonna beat it out.*
> *I mean give that money like I explain to you,*
> *I'm gonna beat it out.*
> *'Cause I heard Frankie Dusen say.*[66]

Although it is difficult to date exactly when Frankie Duson became a regular member of Bolden's band, it was late in Bolden's playing career. For many years Willy Cornish had been Bolden's regular trombone player. A detailed, if not necessarily historically accurate, version of events relating to Duson joining Bolden is attributed to Dude Bottley. The New Orleans guitarist Danny Barker claimed he had interviewed Dude Bottley in the 1950s. Dude Bottley was allegedly the brother of balloonist Buddy Bottley, who worked with Bolden in Lincoln Park. Barker later said he had added "a little monkeyshine" to a story that was "in essence true" and he had "put it together from many accounts collected over the years."[67]

> There were dozens of small string groups and bands and at that time among the most popular were Mr. Charlie Sweet Lovin' Galloway, Punkie Valentin, Señor Butts and Pinchback Touro. Buddy Bolden was the most popular of all, but he was jealous of the great rhythms, showmanship and popularity of Mr. Sweet Lovin' Galloway with his fiddle and mandolin solos, especially since Galloway was a clown and had an engaging personality and a large following. He featured three

terrific horn blowers who loved to battle Bolden's band. They were Edward Clem, cornet; Frankie Dusen [sic], trombone; and Frank Lewis, clarinet. Bolden started scheming and figuring how to break up that band, so he fired Brock Mumford, his guitarist, and clarinetist Willie Warner as well as trombonist Willie Cornish. Then he connived and hired Galloway's men: he hired Frankie Dusen, Frankie Lewis and the banjoist Lorenzo Staultz. When Bolden stole Galloway's key men, he took all the steam and fire out of Sweet Lovin' Galloway's band. Galloway just faded from the picture when these men left.[68]

It is clear that the events Morton described in his lyrics to "Buddy Bolden's Blues" relate to the later years of Bolden's playing career. Judge Fogarty was not presiding in New Orleans until 1904 and Frankie Duson was not a regular member of Bolden's band until around the same time. Morton was probably born in 1890, and would have still been in his early teens when Bolden was at his peak.[69] If he did have firsthand knowledge of Bolden and his band performing "Buddy Bolden's Blues," it would have been later versions of the song. While Morton's lyrics do relate to events late in Bolden's playing career, this in itself does not prove conclusively when this song became a part of Bolden's repertoire.

The other lyric in Morton's version of "Buddy Bolden's Blues" that may help date the song is the stanza:

I thought I heard Buddy Bolden shout,
Open up that window and let that bad air out.
Open up that window and let that foul air out.
I thought I heard Buddy Bolden say.[70]

These lyrics relate to an incident when Bolden was playing at a dance hall in New Orleans. Bolden ordered the windows be opened because the smell was becoming unbearable. The earliest known appearance of this story appeared in Spriggins's articles in the *Louisiana Weekly*. According to this account, the event took place at Odd Fellows Hall, and Willy Cornish was the composer of the subsequent song.[71] Although Spriggins did not publish the actual lyrics, they were probably similar to those recalled by Mrs. Susie Farr. In an interview with Richard Allen she recalled Johnson Park and Lincoln Park, and that the "children in the neighborhood were saying, 'Funky butt, funky butt, take it away.'"[72] At the time, the word "Funky" was a slang term for *smelly*. The song became so popular that one New Orleans venue became known as Funky Butt Hall because of its association with Bolden. However, this was not Odd Fellows Hall, where Cornish told Spriggins that this incident occurred.

Odd Fellows Masonic Hall was a furniture store until 1897 and "it was leased to Jacob Itzkovitch who eventually bought the building in 1904. . . . In 1898, Itzkovitch rented the large upstairs area (entered at 1116 Perdido Street) to the Odd Fellows as a concert hall and meeting room."[73] This would suggest that these events could have taken place at any time from 1898, when the Odd Fellows had the use of the hall. What this does not explain is how the Union Sons Hall, a couple of blocks away down Perdido Street, became known as Funky Butt Hall. According to Donald Marquis:

> Musicians and patrons had other names for Union Sons Hall. After Bolden became its most famous occupant it was popularly known as Funky Butt Hall. Before that its nicknames were "Kenna's Hall," "Kenny's Hall," and "Kinney's Hall," these nicknames quite possibly coming from one of the organization's presidents, William S. Kinney. A 1904 amendment to the Union Sons charter included the minutes of a meeting in which officers were elected, and Kinney, a laborer residing at 627 Liberty, was listed as the new president.[74]

A number of the early jazz musicians who remember Bolden use the names Funky Butt Hall and Kinney's Hall (or one of the variants) interchangeably.[75] Manuel Manetta confirmed in an interview with William Russell that from a time when Frankie Duson was playing with Buddy Bolden "a man named Kenna" operated "Funky Butt Hall."[76] This tends to suggest that it was from a time around or after 1904 when William S. Kinney became the president of the Union Sons Relief Association of Louisiana that the hall became known as Funky Butt Hall, rather than at some earlier date.

It is interesting that Willy Cornish claimed to have written the tune to "Buddy Bolden's Blues." It is less clear if he is responsible for the lyrics.[77] Although "Willy Cornish talked and sang nasty,"[78] Lorenzo Staultz is principally associated with singing "Buddy Bolden's Blues." With due regard for the possibility of a liberal sprinkling of "monkeyshine," according to (the probably fictitious) Dude Bottley:

> Dusen and Bolden used to get a great big happy feeling when Lorenzo sang. He could sing Funky Butt for an hour; he could sing all day and all night if he wanted to, because he would sing about all the notoriety

whores, pimps, madams and even about the policeman at the door. Of course the policeman did not ever hear all the nasty lowdown things that Lorenzo would be singing about him and the police department, the mayor, the governor, the president. He would even sing about the Civil War; about how General Grant made Jeff Davis kiss and kiss his behind and how General Sherman burnt up Georgia riding on Robert E. Lee's back. The crowd would scream and holler but Lorenzo would stand up and sing about them white folks with his eye watching the policeman on the door. The policeman would not know what he would be singing but Lorenzo was protecting his head and taking no chances. One chorus I'll always remember was:

'I thought I heer'd Abe Lincoln shout,
"Rebels, close down them plantations and let them niggers out."
I'm positively sure I heer'd Mr. Lincoln shout.
I thought I heard Mr. Lincoln say,
"Rebels, close down them plantations and let all them niggers out.
You gonna lose the war; git on your knees and pray
You gonna lose the war; git on your knees and pray!"
That's the words I heer'd Mr. Lincoln say.[79]

This could be a reference to "Emancipation Day," a tune that *Jazzmen* claimed was "inspired by some 'low-life'" woman who had worked on a boat with Bolden's band.[80] Despite the coincidence in title, there is no obvious connection between this song and "On Emancipation Day" (1902), a song by Will Marion Cook and Paul Laurence Dunbar, from the musical *In Dahomey.*

There are, however, two published tunes that are similar to "Buddy Bolden's Blues": "The St. Louis Tickle" and "The Cake Walk in the Sky."

In *The Art of Ragtime: Form and Meaning of an Original Black American Art,* William J. Schafer and Johannes Riedel argue that:

The melodies of different strains of a rag are apt to contrast sharply, but they are similar in that they follow lyrical, vocal lines. They can be hummed or sung easily, and they often sound like simple folk songs when isolated from the rag structure. In fact, the melodies often are folk tunes or folk rag themes found in many other contexts (e.g., "Buddy Bolden's Blues" theme which is apparently a levee work song

Example 1: "The St. Louis Tickle" (vocal version, 1905)

and appears in Barney and Seymore's "St. Louis Tickle" and in a half-dozen other ragtime contexts).[81]

The popularity of "The St. Louis Tickle" appears also to have attracted imitators. By 1905 Scott Joplin had published "Sarah Dear," a sentimental love song that bore a striking similarity to "The St. Louis Tickle."[82] Another tune based on the same melody that appeared as sheet music after "The St. Louis Tickle" was Louis Chauvin's ballad "Babe, It's Too Long Off" (1906).

By 1905, lyrics that at least have a passing resemblance to "Buddy Bolden's Blues," inclusive of the "take it away" phrase, were published in a vocal version of "The St. Louis Tickle" (see Ex. 1).

One influential New Orleans bandleader who played "The St. Louis Tickle" was John Robichaux.

In 1905 when black New Orleans was in tune with the new music and Bolden was at his height, his primary rival was John Robichaux, a Creole who nevertheless lived Uptown on Tchoupitoulas Street and competed with Bolden in some of the rougher spots. Robichaux was in many ways the epitome of the New Orleans Creole of Color. Born January 16, 1866, in the bayou county town of Thibodaux, he was older than Bolden and had the advantage of an excellent musical education. When he moved to New Orleans in 1891 he promptly became the drummer for Theogene Baquet's highly regarded Excelsior Cornet Band; shortly thereafter he organized his own band.[83]

Manuel Manetta, as a child, recalled hearing Robichaux's band playing in Lincoln Park in New Orleans.

I heard Robichaux's band when I was still in short pants and attending school. I would borrow my brother's long pants to go to Lincoln Park in Carrollton, where Robichaux's band was the usual attraction. He was the famous band of the town. Dancing at Lincoln Park, held on Sunday, began at 4 pm. The personnel of Robichaux's band which was a full band: Robichaux-violin, Jim Williams-trumpet, Batiste Delisle-trombone, George Baquet-clarinet. The band strictly played from music, including Scott Joplin numbers. The only number they played by ear was 'Home Sweet Home.' The Robichaux Band played in the open weather permitting, from 4 pm until 7 pm. After a break of one hour-for meals, etc. they played in the dance hall at the park from 8 until 4 am.[84]

Bud Scott recalled one of the legendary contests that took place in Lincoln Park between Buddy Bolden and John Robichaux:

I joined John Robichaux in 1904. There were 7 men in the band (no piano). Guitar, violin, Jim Williams was on trumpet (he used to use a mute), Baptiste Delisle on trombone, Dee Dee Chandler on drums and the greatest bass player I ever heard in my life-Henry Kimball. They played for the elite and had the town sewed up. In about 1908 [This date is wrong; Bolden had been committed to Jackson Asylum in June 1907], Robichaux had a contest with Bolden in Lincoln Park and Robichaux for the contest added Manuel Perez. Bolden got hotheaded that night, as Robichaux really had his gang out.[85]

Fortunately, John Robichaux's musical library was donated to the Hogan Jazz Archive. There are 6,092 orchestrations and 1,164 piano scores. This collection shows the evolution of dance and jazz styles from 1877 to the 1940s.[86] One of these arrangements from 1904 is "The St. Louis Tickle," which Morton claimed was "stolen" from Buddy Bolden. "The St. Louis Tickle" was a very popular tune. A stock arrangement, published by the Victor Kremer Company in Chicago, was available to any band that wished to include the number in their repertoire. The *New York Clipper* of November 4, 1905, in a block advertisement for the Kremer Company noted that "The St. Louis Tickle" was a "Rag Time Hit" and was "Absolutely a Novelty in Syncopated Melody, Played by Bands and Orchestras Everywhere," and that it was available "Published as a Song" with "Lyrics by Jim O'Dea."[87] That "The

Example 2: Ben Harney, "The Cakewalk in the Sky" (1899)

St. Louis Tickle" had acquired lyrics by this time is clear from a report in the *Indianapolis Freeman* from a few weeks earlier. It reported on a vaudeville bill from the Pekin Theater, Chicago, saying that "Jimmy Wall pleased everybody singing, the St. Louis Tickle Song and 'Everybody Works But Father.'"[88] Given that Bolden's principal musical rival played "The St. Louis Tickle," this raises the question: did Buddy Bolden learn the tune from Robichaux? If he did, he can only have done so after 1904. If he played his theme song before 1904, it would seem that Jelly Roll Morton could be correct and Theron C. Bennett may indeed have "stolen" Bolden's theme song.

Bennett was a Missouri-born pianist who first published in 1902 and by 1904 was working as a composer and arranger for the Victor Kremer Company. How did he come to know the melody? One credible explanation is that he was already familiar with "The Cake Walk in the Sky" (1899), by Ben Harney.[89]

Ben Harney is perhaps best known for composing "You've Been a Good Old Wagon" (1895). The circumstances surrounding the publication of this song provides insight into Ben Harney's musical background. According to his publisher Bruner Greenup: "It was no trouble for Harney . . . to play this piece according to ragtime principles, but the great difficulty which beset us when we started out to publish the song was to get the 'rag' in print. Harney had no more idea than a monkey how to write rag time, though he could play and sing it better, perhaps, than anyone has ever yet succeeded in doing."[90] Harney was both a composer and performer who worked in vaudeville. By 1899, he was billed as the "Originator of Ragtime."[91] In 1899 Witmark and Sons published "The Cake Walk in the Sky" in two versions: an instrumental in the key of F, described as an "Ethiopian Two-Step" and arranged for piano by F. W. Meacham; and a version in the key of Eb, which included lyrics and a "RAG CHORUS ad lib."

A comparison of the opening bars of the chorus of "The Cake Walk in the Sky" (see Ex. 2) with the version of "Buddy Bolden's Blues," which Jelly Roll Morton published in 1939, confirms that the opening phrase is essentially the same. Rhythmically the only obvious difference is that "The Cake Walk in the Sky" is in quarter notes and "Buddy Bolden's Blues" is in eighth notes. This results in there being two measures of "The Cake Walk in the Sky" for each measure of "Buddy Bolden's Blues." In both cases, the melody descends chromatically (in semitones) from Bb, through A-natural, Ab and G. But, there is an interesting evolution in the harmony of the opening measures of these three related tunes. In "The Cake Walk in the Sky" (m. 5) the harmony moves to Bb-seventh before a return to the tonic chord of Eb in (m. 7). This harmonic move from the tonic chord to the dominant (the fifth degree of the scale) is an example of a perfect cadence. The perfect cadence is the fundamental cadence in European tonal music.[92]

The perfect cadence became a staple of European music making because of the widespread adoption of major scales that replaced the earlier church modes. The scale of Eb-major contains a leading note (D) that is a semitone below the tonic (Eb). Because the leading note is a semitone away from the tonic, the ear recognizes this chromatic dissonance and seeks its resolution. Expressed harmonically the D (the major third of the Bb chord) in the right-hand piano part (m. 6) resolves upward to Eb (m. 7). This chromatic tension is further enhanced because the Bb chord includes the flatted seventh (Ab). The Ab exerts a downward chromatic pressure on the major third (G) of the Eb chord. The perfect cadence exploits the dissonance that is inherent in the major scale. Only notes from the scale are used and consequently there are no accidentals required when writing a perfect cadence.

In "The St. Louis Tickle" (see Ex. 3), the same section (m. 3) is harmonized rather differently. Instead of dominant harmony, subdominant harmony Ab (the fourth degree of the scale) and F-minor on the second degree are employed. Again, there are no accidentals as both of these chords are formed from the notes of the Eb-major scale.

"Buddy Bolden's Blues" also uses the subdominant chord of Ab (m. 3), but this is followed with an A-diminished-seventh chord in "Buddy Bolden's Blues" (see Ex. 4).

Example 3: Barney and Seymore, "The St. Louis Tickle" (1904)

Example 4: Jelly Roll Morton, "Buddy Bolden's Blues" (1939). "Buddy Bolden's Blues," Words and Music by Ferd "Jelly Roll" Morton, © 1939, 1940, 1950 TEMPO MUSIC PUBLISHING Co. © Renewed EDWIN H. MORRIS & COMPANY, A Division of MPL Music Publishing, Inc. All Rights Reserved. Reprinted with Permission of Hal Leonard Corporation.

The chord of A-diminished-seventh contains two notes that are not in the key of E♭-major (G♭ and A-natural) and these notes, therefore, have accidentals. One of these, the G♭, is the minor third of the key. This is the hallmark of blues tonality. In composed blues, it is common for melodies (and the harmony) to contain both major and minor thirds. In "Buddy Bolden's Blues" a minor third is employed (mm. 3, 4, 5, 6, 7, 11, 13, and 15), whereas this interval appears only once per chorus of Harney's composition, and three times in "The St. Louis Tickle."

If Jelly Roll Morton's rendition of "Buddy Bolden's Blues" is an accurate representation of the music that Bolden played, then we have a clear example of a ragtime tune, which (to use the language of Carl Engel) was "relished with spicier" harmony.[93] Moreover, this harmony shows the clear imprint of blues tonality. Rhythmically, "Buddy Bolden's Blues" as recorded by Morton is in 4/4 time rather than the 2/4 time of a rag. In terms of form, there is a simple chorus that is repeated, and this was played, and sung, by a group of musicians led by a cornet player rather than a violinist.

There are no surviving recordings of Buddy Bolden and his band, and skeptics may well question the extent to which Morton's recollections accurately reflect the music of Buddy Bolden. By the time Morton recorded this tune in the late 1930s this kind of tonality was well established. In the absence of a more credible witness, the issue of whether Bolden played jazz cannot be resolved. But in fact, there is a more credible witness: a man who played with the Bolden band and who described in some detail Bolden's style of playing.

3

 JUST BUNK?

IT HAS NOT BEEN EASY FOR JAZZ RESEARCHERS TO DECIDE WHAT CRED-
ibility to give to William Geary "Bunk" Johnson. He had undeniable musical
ability, but his cavalier attitude to dates reflected badly on his reputation as
a reliable witness to the early years of jazz in New Orleans.

The *Jazzmen* authors first heard of Bunk Johnson through New Orleans
soprano saxophonist Sidney Bechet. He described Bunk as "one of the three
great trumpet players in jazz." Given that he cited Buddy Bolden and Louis
Armstrong as the other two, this was high praise.[1] Louis Armstrong seemed
to have agreed with Bechet and advised, "The fellow they [the *Jazzmen* au-
thors] ought to write about is Bunk. Man, what a man! They should talk
about that man . . . that alone."[2]

In 1939, Bunk was located working in a rice mill in New Iberia. He no
longer had a cornet; his front teeth were missing, and he no longer played.
He was earning just $1.75 a day driving a truck.[3] There was a powerful in-
centive for Bunk to tell his story, and he had little to lose if he exaggerated
things a little. This may explain why he assured the *Jazzmen* authors: "King
Bolden and myself were the first men that began playing jazz in the city of
dear old New Orleans. . . . So you tell them all that Bunk and King Bolden's
Band was the first ones that started jazz in the City or any place else. And
now you are able to go ahead with your book."[4]

Here was an opportunity to get his teeth fixed, get a cornet, and earn
some money. The *Jazzmen* authors were willing to help with this. Sidney
Bechet's brother, Leonard, was a dentist and would do the work on his teeth.
A collection was made to get Bunk a cornet. Finally, Bunk Johnson would be
recognized as a jazz pioneer.

He told the *Jazzmen* authors that he was born December 27, 1879, and
that around the age of fifteen he began playing with Adam Olivier's band.
The Olivier band was a reading band, but by this time, Bunk thought himself as "hard to beat" for "playing by head."[5] He claimed that his chance came

to prove his abilities when, after a year with Olivier, he got an opportunity to join Bolden's band.

> So I told Mr. Olivier that I think I could do better with King Bolden so he told me to suit myself and so I did and went on with King Bolden in the year of 1895. When I started playing with him Bolden was a married man and two children. He must have been between 25 or 30 years old at the time. Now here are the men in the band when I went in to it: Cornelius Tilman, drummer, Willy Cornish, trombone, Bolden, cornet, Bunk, cornet, Willie Warner, clarinet, Mumford, guitar, and Jimmy Johnson, bass. That was the old Bolden band when I went in it. They were all men; I was the only young one in the Band, in short pants.[6]

Bolden was born in 1877.[7] Bunk Johnson claimed to have been born in 1879; whenever he joined the band, there should only have been a small difference in age between them. However, Bunk consistently said that Bolden was older than he was. In an article that appeared in 1946, Bunk provided further details of his first encounter with the Bolden band.

> He was playing a job in Lincoln Park with the Olivier Band. The famous Buddy Bolden was playing just two blocks away at Johnson Park. The two bands had their respective crowds and fans. Soon the trumpet of Bolden started "callin' his chillun home." Since the Olivier band could not compete with its rival the musicians had to call it a day and go home. But not Bunk. Being curious to see for himself just how good the Bolden men were, he wandered over into the enemy territory. He looked for the music racks and to his surprise couldn't find any. These musicians were playing without music! Bunk had his cornet in a green cloth bag (made from a pool table covering by his loving mother) and it was tied with a bright red ribbon. This was to keep his instrument from being scratched. The mighty Bolden looked down at the slim youth standing in awe before him and said, "What's that you got in that bag, boy?"[8]

Bunk told him it was a cornet and that he could play the blues in any key.[9] Bolden then wandered off to get a drink leaving Bunk to play with the band.

Bunk consistently said that he first played with Bolden in Johnson Park. From this, we can be sure that he did not play with Bolden in 1895, because

Johnson Park and neighboring Lincoln Park opened for business in 1902. If, as Bunk said, he first played with Olivier in Lincoln Park and then with the Bolden band in Johnson Park, he had also provided the earliest possible date when this could have occurred.

On March 31, 1902, George W. Johnson petitioned the council of New Orleans to carry on the business of operating a baseball park on two blocks in the Seventh District "bounded by Short, Forshey, Oleander and Burdette Street."[10] It is not clear how long it took George W. Johnson to develop the site and make it ready for baseball games. It seems likely that he could have opened for business soon after, possibly in time for the summer season of 1902. From the City Directory we know that, by 1904, George W. Johnson ran a saloon on the corner of Short and Oleander.[11] It seems reasonable to suppose that George Johnson would have wasted little time in getting this saloon into operation. It was in this saloon that Bunk claimed to have played with the Bolden band.

In 1974, to get information for his book on Buddy Bolden, Fred and Amelia Ramsey interviewed Ferrand and Mathilda Clementine. They lived at 3300 Fern Street just across from where Johnson Park had been. Ferrand described the "dance hall" as "one of them old time buildings" where they used to dance the quadrille and "raise sin."[12] He described the venue as being around sixty feet long and the width of a double fronted house.[13]

It is possible that George Johnson built the saloon before he petitioned for the baseball park. Ferrand Clementine was born on Christmas Day 1894 and moved to the area at the age of five. At the time, the house was under construction and he recalled playing on the site; the carpenters, he remembered, would chase him away. He also said "old man Johnson" lived "right there—he lived right in the park where he built it." At the time, it was the only building.[14]

The house had wooden pilings and a wooden floor. It had a flat front with no porch. The band would play in the back corner of the building. In this corner there was a window, and it was from this window that "Buddy Bolden would put his horn out the back, and the other band over on Lincoln Park—their band would be there, and one would try to out-blow one another—playing music."[15] Willy Cornish confirmed that Johnson Park was the park they played most often. He also confirmed they would "stick horns out [the] window in [the] direction of Lincoln Park, where Robichaux played."[16]

From this we can be reasonably sure that, if Bunk did play with Bolden, it was after 1902 and when he was still quite young. This later date is compatible with the repertoire that Bunk recalled. Bunk said that when he joined Bolden they played "The St. Louis Tickle," "Didn't He Ramble," "Sammy Samson," "Lazy Moon," and "Bowery Buck," along with quadrilles and "all kinds of blues."[17] As discussed earlier, "The St. Louis Tickle" was published in 1904; "Oh! Didn't He Ramble" appeared as sheet music in 1902, with words and music by Will Handy; "Sammy Samkins" was a march and two-step by C. E. Billings, published in 1902; "Lazy Moon" by Bob Cole appeared in 1903; and "Bowery Buck," by the ragtime composer Tom Turpin, received copyright in 1899. All of these tunes could have been played by Buddy Bolden—but not in 1895 as Bunk originally claimed.

Because much of the information about early New Orleans jazz contained in *Jazzmen* rested on the word of Bunk Johnson, his date of birth has become a topic of considerable interest to jazz researchers. In writing *Jazzmen* the contributors didn't know Bolden's date of birth, nor did they have the benefit of nearly seventy years of jazz research. Today, it is easy to question why the *Jazzmen* editors accepted Bunk's testimony with what appears to have been so little scrutiny. However, in fairness, they were hearing this for the first time and were unable to check much that they were told. It is clear through Fred Ramsey's correspondence that in hindsight the *Jazzmen* authors did accept that they would have been wise to check their sources with more caution. Fred Ramsey wrote to Bill Russell in later years confiding that they had "all had plenty of time to regret" rushing into print with *Jazzmen*.[18]

Given that Bunk's date of birth became central to issues surrounding the authority of *Jazzmen*, it is perhaps understandable that Bunk's date of birth became almost an article of faith for Bill Russell. As Mike Hazeldine noted, "if one dared to hint that maybe, perhaps, it might not be 1879, then you were not going to escape without a severe lecture. And yet . . . going through Bill's papers after he died, he had kept all of the evidence which might suggest otherwise."[19]

Researchers have attempted to locate documents that would confirm Bunk Johnson's date of birth.[20] Dates that have been found in official documents include 1879 in the 1930 census and on a 1949 wedding application; 1880 on his death certificate; 1882 on his 1918 draft card; 1885 on his two wedding certificates (in 1907 and 1949); and 1889 on a 1937 social security application.[21] Bunk was inconsistent throughout his life in recording his date of birth, and in all probability he did not know when he was born. December 27, 1889, is believed his most likely date of birth; this is based principally on Lawrence Gushee's article in the *Jazz Archivist* (vol. II, no. 2, November 1987), "When Was Bunk Born and Why Should We Care?"[22] Gushee located an entry for "Gerry Johnson" (b. December 1889) in the 1900 Federal Census. He lived at 3523 Tchoupitoulas Street with his mother, Theresa Johnson (b. May 1856), and his sister Regalia (b. July 1878). The only other member of the household was Theresa's mother-in-law, Millis Young (b. 1845).

Gushee thought that this was likely to be Bunk because he had a middle name "Gerry" or "Geary"; his mother's name was Theresa; she was a cook (in the census record), and according to Bunk she had at least three different food outlets in the Tchoupitoulas area: "My mother operated three restaurants. One place was located on Tchoupitoulas on the corner of N. Peters and Conti Street. The second was between 4th St. and Washington Street on Tchoupitoulas, and the third was located on Tchoupitoulas and St James, across from the Empire Rice Mill."[23]

If this is William Geary "Bunk" Johnson, his age and date of birth have been entered incorrectly. This is not as unlikely as it sounds. Gushee noted that Gerry's age has been altered on the census and his date of birth has been written in the hand of someone other than the main census taker.[24] A further inconsistency is that both Gerry and his sister Regalia are recorded as being "at school." If Regalia's date of birth was given correctly, she was still attending school at the age of twenty-one. But there are other reasons to think Gerry's birth date had been entered incorrectly. The date of 1889 is simply incompatible with the verifiable evidence surrounding Bunk's early years.

Of one thing we can be certain: Theresa Johnson in the 1900 census is Bunk's mother. Bunk gave two different names for his father. He was either called William or Gary (Gerry). The Soards' City Directory for New Orleans records that a Garry Johnson, a laborer, was living at 743 Annunciation in 1891. The same address for Theresa Johnson and Jeremiah Johnson appeared in 1892. It seems that Garry or Gerry was a contraction of his father's name. We can be sure that this is the same Theresa Johnson to appear in the 1900 census because Millie Young (her mother-in-law in the 1900 census) also lived at 743 Annunciation in 1892.[25]

Bunk Johnson said that his father died in 1886, which (given he claimed in *Jazzmen* to have been born in 1879) is compatible with him also saying that he was seven years old when his father died. Because we know that Jeremiah Johnson was Bunk's father, it is also possible to show that Bunk's father died five years later than Bunk claimed. In 1892 Jeremiah and Theresa Johnson lived together at 743 Annunciation. The 1893 Soards' entry records that Theresa was still at the same address and was the "widow of Jeremiah." So Jeremiah must have died late in 1892 or early in 1893. If Bunk was born in

December 1889 as the 1900 census suggests, then Bunk was little more than a baby when his father died.[26]

According to Bunk, around the age of six he went to live with his maternal grandmother, Rosa Jefferson, at Tchoupitoulas between Valmont and Bellecastle. It was from here that, according to Bunk, he began his schooling at New Orleans University.

The Methodist Church founded New Orleans University on March 22, 1873. The charter states that New Orleans University, "in the matter of receiving and instructing students, shall make no distinction as to race, color, sex, or religious belief."[27] In September 1884 the Freedmen's Aid Society purchased a site on St. Charles Avenue between Valmont and Leontine Streets; the block behind was added three years later.[28] It is here that Bunk claimed to have learned to play the cornet: "I learned to play cornet when I was attending New Orleans University. I learned to play cornet under Prof. Cutchey Wallace. He was our teacher at New Orleans University and also our organist in chapel and he's the one that taught me cornet and learned me music. And I taken lessons from him from the age of six years old until I finished New Orleans University."[29]

New Orleans University did offer music lessons. The yearbook for 1880–81 states: "Lessons on the organ or piano, including use of instruments, are given for $3 per month. Instruction in vocal culture is given to all free of charge."[30] By 1897, the cost of music lessons was $1 per month; this was still a considerable sum of money.[31]

From its beginning, the university published yearbooks listing the students and teachers. Researchers have searched in vain for Bunk Johnson's name and that of Cutchey Wallace in these yearbooks.[32] The reason for both Bunk and his teacher being absent from the university's years books is very simple: Bunk did not attend New Orleans University. When in less boastful mood, he confided that his school was *behind* New Orleans University:

When I started going to school at the age 6 we lived on Tchoupitoulas between Bellecastle St & Valmont St. I attended the Baptist School. Now that was the building back of N. O. U. located on St Charles Ave between Leontine and Valmont St. My oldest sister, Maggie took me to school until I learned the way. . . . I always carried a tin bucket to school filled with red beans, rice, cabbage & a glass of syrup.

Every day at 11:45 we had 15 min at the chapel with Prof. Wallace Cutchey. He was Mexican who played the chapel organ & gave us our music lessons. I learned the rudiments of music 1st & then singing. I sang four yrs before I touched an instrument.

We had two days a week devoted to studying an instrument. Mr. Cutchey taught me how to play cornet. I played in the school band which played all street marches, overtures and waltzes. This school band was used to play at all the ball games.[33]

New Orleans University was Methodist. Bunk made clear that his school was Baptist, and it was "back of" New Orleans University. The Robinson fire insurance map of 1883 shows a school on Constance Street between Leontine and Valmont. This is directly behind, although many blocks, from New Orleans University. Although the school is on the 1883 map, there are dwellings on the site in 1896.[34] Given that it is likely Bunk attended school until around 1899 (or later), this is probably not Bunk's school. Another school was St. Francis Industrial School at 72 Valmont Street (under the old numbering system). Again, this is unlikely to be Bunk's school. As the name suggests, this was probably a Catholic school under the direction of Sister Mary Bernette.[35]

A place where Bunk could have taken his music lessons was Beulah Baptist Church, two blocks from where Bunk lived, heading away from the river and toward New Orleans University. Beulah Baptist Church was established by Ezekiel Warmington. He had settled in New Orleans in 1890 at 738 Laurel, and at the time gave his occupation as "laborer."[36] In the following years he established "Bula Church (colored)" at (under the new numbering system) 5240 Laurel, between Valmont and Bellecastle.[37] The 1896 City Directory records the pastor as the Rev. E. K. Wymington [sic] who gave this address as his place of residence.[38] City directories and census returns reveal nothing about Bunk's music teacher Cutchey Wallace. Bunk did, however, say that he took lessons "with the sexton Coochie Wallace."[39] This would suggest that he was not only the chapel organist, but also the caretaker of Beulah Baptist Church. Bunk said: "My Prof. was a Mexican; his name was Mr. Wallace Cutchey. He told me that I had a long way to go and a short time to make it in. Boy I got busy and really made the grade. When I became the age of 15 yrs old I was good to go and I really have been going ever since."[40] Beulah Baptist Church is listed in Soards' City Directory until 1902. There is no pastor in this final entry.[41] Maps and directories show no other Baptist church or chapel in the area. It seems likely that was where Bunk Johnson took his music lessons. If he did, he can only have done so between the early 1890s and 1902, as by this time the church had closed.

Bunk consistently told enquirers that he left school the year before the Robert Charles Riot. In 1944, Robert Goffin visited New Orleans to research *La Nouvelle-Orléans Capital du Jazz* (1946). For the book, he interviewed Bunk Johnson. Bunk mistakenly believed that the Robert Charles Riot took place in 1895 rather than July 1900. He said that Bolden was playing with Billy Peyton and "Big Eye" Louis Nelson at the time of the Riot, and that he had left university a year earlier in 1894; he believed that the beginnings of syncopated music also dated from the same year as the riots. This, Goffin realized, explained why Bunk had dated Bolden's commitment to a mental institution to 1903 rather than the actual date of 1907; his erroneous belief that the Riot had taken place five years earlier than it had caused Bunk to date other events earlier than they had actually occurred.[42]

This explains the anomaly in Bunk's dating of events. Because Bunk believed the Riot took place in 1895, he simply adjusted his dates and age to suit. Bunk told the *Jazzmen* authors that he was born December 1879. If we assume that his actual birth date was five years later than this—December 1884—we now have a consistent narrative that is completely compatible with the available evidence. At around the age of seven (1892) his father died; at around this time, or perhaps a year earlier (when he would have been six), he began his schooling at Beulah Baptist Church, which had just been established by the Reverend Warmington. He would have celebrated his fifteenth birthday in December 1899. If we assume that he was playing with Adam Olivier in 1902, when Lincoln and Johnson parks opened, Bunk would have been around seventeen or eighteen at the time of his encounter with Bolden in Johnson Park. He would still have been in short pants, as the custom at the time was for boys to wear short pants until they were twenty-one.

This also explains some of Bunk's later recollections and the dates he gave. Bunk claimed to have played with Jelly Roll Morton in "Hattie Rogers' sporting house in 1903." Bunk remembered, "She had a whole lot of light-colored women in there, best-looking women you ever want to see."[43]

For many years Morton's date of birth was as uncertain as Bunk Johnson's. As Alan Lomax noted, in interviewing Morton for his book *Mister Jelly Roll: The Fortunes of Jelly Roll Morton, New Orleans Creole and "Inventor of Jazz"*: "Jelly Roll could juggle his age as it suited him—writing 1888 on his insurance policy, giving 1885 on the Library of Congress records since this year put him in Storyville earlier than most other jazz men and gave him plenty of historical elbow room, and telling his wife the year was 1886."[44] Lawrence Gushee found Morton's baptismal certificate and his most likely date of birth is October 20, 1890.[45] It is therefore very unlikely that Morton was playing in "sporting houses" at the age of thirteen. Morton's own recollections indicate that he first began working in the District for Hilma Burt in 1907. Morton recalled, "At the age of 17 I went around to gambling houses." Morton then tells of how the piano player in one of the houses became sick: "[I was asked] would I like to make a few dollars. I went there to sing and play. They had a legitimate white pianist there—nothing hot. I went in there and started on the job. In a week I had plenty of money in my pocket. Miss Burt asked me if I wanted to work steady. 'If you think you can come steady, I will be glad to have you. Everybody likes your work very much.'"[46] Morton went on to say, "There was a slump and they had some kind of draft checks around. Drafts were as good as a gold dollar. At this time, working in small time sporting houses and they would call you when they needed you."[47] This relates to the Wall Street Panic of 1907, when large withdrawals caused banks to issue bonds to protect their currency reserves. The height of the run on the banks took place in October 1907.[48]

The other thing that suggests that Morton and Johnson did not play together in the District until 1907 is that Bunk said that he was playing with Frankie Duson's Eagle Band at the same time. "Sometimes after I'd knock off at four in the morning, Jelly would ask me to come over and play with him— he'd play and sing the blues till way up in the day."[49] Frankie Duson did not take over the leadership of the Eagle Band until after Buddy Bolden ceased playing, which was probably toward the end of 1906.

Among Fred Ramsey's papers, there is an arrest report from 1903 that would also support the view that Bunk Johnson was born earlier than 1889. Ramsey found a report of a "general disturbance of the peace" at a ball hosted by the Ladies' Broadway Swells at the uptown "Odd Fellows' and Masonic Hall," on Perdido near Rampart Street in the early hours of Tuesday March 10, 1903. From the subsequent court case, it emerges that a bystander had been shot in a dispute over a handkerchief that belonged to Frank Bush. At the court hearing, Anthony Clark described the events that led to the killing of Manuel Hostler: "I was sitting at the music stand and the quadrille was going on, Hostler was in between Frank Bush and the music stand, and the shooting took place just a little before the quadrille started. I saw the shot fired and Hostler fell. He was close to Frank Bush. Hostler was standing close to the music stand."[50] In the ensuing panic, it was impossible for the police to determine what had happened, and they decided to arrest all those who had not already fled the scene. The following morning the police recorded all of the names and addresses of the more than one hundred people they had arrested. They were all "colored" and all gave uptown addresses. None of those arrested gave their occupation as musician; but among those arrested who may have been musicians were the 24-year-old "cooper" Albert Carroll (208 Broadway); Tony Jackson, a 21-year-old laborer who lived at 3920 Magazine Street; Frank Richards, a laborer residing at 1208 Tchoupitoulas, and William Johnson, a 23-year-old servant living at 5272 Tchoupitoulas. Ramsey believed that this was Bunk Johnson.[51] It is striking that 5272 Tchoupitoulas Street is in the block where Bunk said he lived as a child with his grandmother, "on Tchoupitoulas between Bellecastle St & Valmont St."[52]

While we cannot be certain that this is Bunk, there is much that suggests that it is. We know that he became a regular at the Odd Fellows Hall and knew Tony Jackson. Bunk remembered: "Tony Jackson started playing piano by ear in Adam Olivier's tonk on the corner of Amelia and Tchoupitoulas. That was between 1892 and 1893."[53] They also played together in Adam Olivier's band. This is very likely to have been before 1904, when Tony Jackson began touring with the Whitman Sisters, returning from time to time to New Orleans. It is said that "the singing of Tony Jackson and Baby Alice Whitman usually brought down the house."[54] While we cannot be certain that this William Johnson was Bunk, we can be sure that this is the piano player Tony Jackson. His entry in the 1903 Soards' City Directory records Tony Jackson, a "musician" at 3920 Magazine Street. William Johnson is an extremely common name; therefore, we cannot completely rule out the possibility that there were two William Johnsons who lived on Tchoupitoulas between Valmont and Bellecastle around the turn of the century and who both frequented Odd Fellows Hall; however, the statistical probability is slight.

If Bunk Johnson was among those arrested at Odd Fellows Hall in 1903, of course it does not follow that he was 23 years old. It would be necessary to persuade the police that he was old enough to be there. It does, however, cast doubt on an 1889 birth date. While it may be possible for someone in their late teenage years to pass for twenty-three, it is simply not credible that someone in their early teens could succeed in such a deception.

Once we accept the possibility that Bunk was born in December 1884 (or a year either side), and a corresponding correction is factored in, the remaining anomalies can be reconciled. An example of this is a letter from Joe "King" Oliver to Bunk Johnson in 1930.[55] Oliver wrote, "I'm sure you will be kind enough to admit that I'm a few years younger than you are. I know you remember when I used to come around and listen to you play."[56]

The problem is that there is widespread belief that Joe Oliver was born in Abend, a few miles from Donaldsonville, on December 19, 1885. He should, taking Johnson's date of birth as December 27, 1889, be four years older, not a "few years younger."

While it is, of course, possible that Oliver was mistaken about their respective ages, the other complication is that Oliver's date of birth is also uncertain. No birth certificate has been found for Joe Oliver and official documents give various dates. Joe and Stella Oliver were married on July 13, 1911; their wedding certificate gives his age as twenty-three.[57] The next official document to give Joe Oliver's date of birth was his registration papers for World War I. The date of birth he gave the registration board was December 19, 1881. There is no doubt that this is the correct Joseph Oliver because he was registered in Chicago, his wife's name is given as Stella, his occupation is "musician," and the scar that he received over his left eye in an accident as a child is noted. Just two years later, in the 1920 census, he was in Chicago with his wife and daughter Ruby. In this document, Joe's age is 35 (i.e., b. ca. 1885); Stella is 33, and Ruby 13. Ruby was therefore probably born in 1908, three years before they married. This is consistent with a remark Stella made that Ruby was her daughter but not Joe's.[58] Later official documents give Joe Oliver's age as compatible with being born in 1885, and his death certificate (in 1938) confirms 1885. In the absence of a birth certificate or an earlier census, it seems unlikely that official documentation will resolve the question of when Joe Oliver was born. However, there is sufficient doubt to make inquiry of his early playing career worthwhile.

Edmond Souchon (who would go on to co-author *New Orleans Jazz: A Family Album* with Al Rose), believed that Joe Oliver's playing career may have started around 1902. At the time Souchon was "four or five" years old, and his African American nanny, Tine, took him "walking into the dense Negro neighborhood to hear Joe Oliver play."[59] By 1907 the young Ed Souchon was making his own way into the city. On one occasion, disguised as newspaper carriers, he and a friend made their way to the "Big 25" where Oliver was playing. According to this account, Oliver was already a bandleader. The deception paid off and they persuaded Oliver to get them in to listen to him play.[60] If Joe Oliver were born in 1885 this would be consistent with a normal musical development; he could well have begun playing in his late teens and have been leading a band in his early twenties. However, those who knew Oliver at this time dispute that he was playing in the early years of the century.

One source of information on Oliver's early years was his wife, Stella. Joe Oliver's mother died sometime around 1900 and he subsequently came to New Orleans where he worked and lived at 2502 Magazine Street at the home of Jacob Levy.[61] Levy & Gonsenheim was a shirt manufacturing company. According to Stella, he worked as a "yard boy." The company is in the New Orleans City Directory from 1904. Stella Dominique (as she was at the time) worked and lived two doors around the corner on Second Street. Stella remembered that when she first met Joe he had lived in New Orleans "several years before that."[62] At the time he was just beginning to learn to play cornet, but he had previously played trombone. Stella said, "Joe was only a boy in short pants when he traveled with the band in which he played trombone." On one occasion the band could not get home from Baton Rouge; "they almost had to walk back."[63] This was a band led by a man identified as "Kenchen." The guitarist Clarence "Little Dad" Vincent said that he knew Joe Oliver when they "first had an organized band. A fellow by the name of Kenchen had all the youngsters from 15 to 18 years old playing in a brass band."[64] George Alfred McCullum also played in this band. George's widow, Bertha, claimed George "taught Joe, and Joe played in his brass band."[65] While this claim may simply be the result of envy, given Joe's success as a jazz pioneer, it cannot be completely discounted either. The significance is that George was born between 1883 and 1885.[66] It would follow from this, if Joe were born in 1885, that he took lesson from a near contemporary.

Bill Russell interviewed Bunk Johnson and asked about his connection to Joe Oliver. Bunk said, "Joe started with old man Kenchen." After Kenchen died, he said, the band was taken over by the cornet player George McCullen [sic]. At the time Joe could "play very little on the cornet."[67] He went on to say that then he and the drummer Walter Brundy (b. 1883)[68] would visit Joe Oliver at "Second and Magazine where Joe was working, and I used to teach Joe there. I used to help Joe. Joe used to follow me in all the parades."[69]

Joe Oliver and Stella were married "four or five years" after they first met. This would suggest they met around 1906. Stella said when they met, Joe was around seventeen years of age, and she was "just a few years younger than Joe."[70] She said, "I was young and he was young. Joe's only two years older than me," and that he was not a musician before she met him. The likelihood is that Oliver either was younger than official documents state or was a late developer as a musician. Whichever is the case, he began playing some years after Bunk Johnson had already begun to develop a reputation as a cornet player, which was why Oliver listened to him play and may even have taken lessons from him. It also seems that it was after Bolden was committed in June 1907 that Oliver came to listen to Johnson and the "Eagle Band every Saturday night."[71] Even if we accept that Johnson was born December 1884 and Oliver December 1885, Johnson would have been just a year older than Joe Oliver, but in terms of musical development he was several years ahead.

The question of when Bunk Johnson was born has particular significance because of his claim to have played with Buddy Bolden. Many prominent musicians disputed this claim. Jelly Roll Morton did much to promote the legend of Buddy Bolden, but he was adamant: "Bunk Johnson, did not play with Buddie Bolden, & wasn't known in the time. Bolden was a blue's [sic] & ragtime player, knew nothing of jazz."[72] Morton, however, had a motive for saying this. He had claimed that he was the "inventor" of jazz in 1902.[73] It followed from this that Bunk Johnson—who claimed to have started jazz with Buddy Bolden—needed to be discredited. Bunk, for his part, also dismissed Morton's claim in a letter to David Stuart: "Now Mr. Stuart you asked me was Jelly Roll Morton one of the first piano players that play jass? No he was not. We had two before Jelly Roll. Tony Jackson was the first piano player that played jass; Harrison Ford was second." Other informants also doubted Bunk's claims regarding Bolden. Willie Santiago said he did not "remember" Bunk playing with Bolden; Sidney Bechet said, "He might have played a piece, or something, with him, but not regular."[74]

The assumption has been that the reports that appeared in *Jazzmen* regarding Bunk playing with Bolden originated with Johnson himself, and that there was no corroboration from any reliable informant. Again, it is the interviews for *Jazzmen* that present the most compelling evidence that Bunk not only sat in with Bolden's band occasionally, but that he played with them on a regular basis. The one informant who had undisputed knowledge of the Bolden band was Willy Cornish. Charles Edward Smith noted from his interview with Willy Cornish during Mardi Gras of 1939: "Bunk put on long pants to go out with Bolden band. Bunk wasn't taught by Bolden and Cornish couldn't remember who it was. Whoever it was, used to smack the cornet out of Bunk's mouth (the guy who smacked him was also a band leader and implication was he'd do this when they were playing, whereever [sic] it was)—smack the horn out of Bunk's mouth to teach him to play right notes."[75] The phrase to "go out" with the Bolden band does suggest that he was an invited guest, rather than a casual player who sat in. At no time did Bunk ever claim he was a pupil of Buddy Bolden, and Cornish confirmed this. Two possible candidates for the bandleader who knocked the cornet out of Bunk's mouth are Cutchey Wallace, who led the boys' band that Bunk played in, or perhaps the man that Bunk called Adam Olivier.

As Lynn Abbott has noted, "Relying on Bunk's oral testimony, historians cast Oleavia as a 'second rate musician' who only played 'stock arrangements.' They also painted him as a downtown Catholic Creole with a French last name—Olivier—when actually he was a Twelfth Ward Baptist American whose name was originally spelled *O'Leavia*."[76]

> Between 1904 and 1911, Adam Oleavia ran a barbershop at 514 General Taylor Street, two blocks from Second Zion Church. Before that, he had a saloon on Tchoupitoulas Street, three blocks from the church. Since the turn of the century, his band had been playing for neighborhood "lawn parties" in a sort of park behind "Smith Row," in the 700 block on Amelia Street—one block from the Second Zion—where there was a bandstand and an area paved for dancing. Two of Oleavia's children played in the band: drummer Tom Oleavia, who was also a barber, and vocalist Celestine Oleavia Burrell, who emulated the great Black Patti. Another daughter, Violet, married a Cato who reportedly played in the Eagle Band.[77]

Perhaps Bunk did not make as decisive a break as he claimed from the Oleavia band. He may have played with Bolden while continuing to learn from Oleavia for a while.

Bunk claimed that the first number that he played with Adam Oleavia's band "when he got out of school" was "Old Popularity."[78] He claimed that he joined the band before Tony Jackson did. At the time, Adam Oleavia was first violin, and Tommy Oleavia, his second son, played second violin; George Pembleton played trombone; George Caldwell, clarinet; Ned Knute and Bunk Johnson, cornet. The bass player was Charles Bazile, Fabbion Kattos played guitar, and Kattos's brother, whose first name he did not give, played drums.[79]

While it is possible that Cornish told Charles Smith about Bunk in response to leading questions, the level of detail indicates that he knew Bunk well. Cornish gave an accurate account of Bunk's style of playing, and this was some three years before Bunk made any recordings: "Bunk's fingering, when he was going good, was easy and sharp. Some of the things Bunk would play, if you'd write it, Bunk would say, 'Do you think I'm a fool; I can't play that.'"[80]

The testimony of Willy Cornish puts the question beyond reasonable doubt: Bunk Johnson played with Buddy Bolden. Bunk, by all accounts—including his own—had to put on long pants to play with Bolden. Bunk can only have played with Bolden sometime after the opening of Johnson and Lincoln Park in 1902. Again this argues persuasively for Bunk being born in 1884. In the end, Bunk's date of birth is only significant because there has been considerable doubt about whether Bunk played with Bolden. It is clear from Cornish's testimony that Bunk did play with Bolden. This rather turns the argument on its head. As he did play with Bolden, it therefore follows that he must have been old enough to have done so.

4

CRACKING-UP A CHORD

AS LONG AGO AS 1930, PERCIVAL R. KIRBY ARGUED IN "A STUDY OF Negro Harmony" that spirituals showed evidence of African harmonic features. More recently Gerhard Kubik has suggested that "jazz harmony at its structural and aesthetic level is based predominantly on African matrices."[1] It is beyond the scope of this book to attempt to trace the harmonic practices of the spirituals and jazz back to Africa, but it can be shown how African American vocal practices of the late nineteenth century related to New Orleans jazz.

An early report of African Americans singing together comes from Frederika Bremer, who traveled through Virginia in 1851. "I first heard the slaves, about a hundred in number, singing at their work in large rooms; they sung quartets . . . in such perfect harmony, and with such exquisite feeling, that it was difficult to believe them self-taught."[2] It is evident from this that when they sang "quartets," it was not four singers but rather in four parts. A few years later Frederick L. Olmstead, in *A Journey in the Seaboard Slave States 1853–54*, wrote: "The common plantation negroes or deck hands of the steamboats will often in rolling cotton bales or carrying wood on board the boat fall to singing, each taking a different part and carrying it on with great spirit and independence and in perfect harmony as I never heard singers who had been considerably educated at the North."[3] In *Slave Songs of the United States* (1867) the editors observed:

> The leading singer starts the words of each verse, often improvising, and the others, who "base" him, as it is called, strike in with the refrain, or even join in the solo, when the words are familiar. . . . And the "basers" themselves seem to follow their own whims, beginning when they please and leaving off when they please, striking an octave above or below (in case they have pitched the tune too low or too high), or hitting some other note that chords, so as to produce the effect of

a marvelous complication and variety, and yet with the most perfect
time, and rarely any discord.[4]

As William Allen conceded in the preface to *Slave Songs*, "the intonation
and variation of even one singer cannot be reproduced on paper. I despair
of conveying any notion of the effect of a number singing together."[5] It was
therefore decided, "As the Negroes have no part-singing, we have thought it
best to print only the melody; what appears only in some places as harmony
is really variations in single notes."[6] As a consequence, we have no reliable
evidence of how African Americans harmonized.

Before the publication of Lynn Abbott's "Play That Barbershop Chord:
A Case for the African American Origin of Barber Shop Harmony" (1992),
it was widely believed that barbershop harmony was principally a white
musical tradition. Instead, Abbott convincingly argues that, by the 1890s
and early 1900s, "for the male population, at least, . . . [barbershop] was
nothing less than a black national pastime."[7] Billy McClain, who worked in
vaudeville, recalled that in Kansas City in the late 1880s, "'about every four
dark faces you met was a quartet."[8] James Weldon Johnson and J. Rosamond
Johnson, writing in *The Book of American Negro Spirituals* (1925), stated:
"Pick up four colored boys or young men anywhere and the chances are
ninety out of a hundred that you have a quartet. Let one of them sing the
melody and the others will naturally find the parts. Indeed, it may be said
that all male Negro youth of the United States is divided into quartets."[9]

Barbershop seventh chords are fundamental to barbershop singing. A
barbershop seventh chord is a simple major triad that is extended to include
the flatted seventh. For example, a simple triad of C-major (C-E-G) would
be extended to include the flatted seventh note (C- E-G-B♭). This chord cannot be formed using the notes of the C-major scale as B♭ is not in the scale
of C-major; it would be necessary to add an accidental (a flat sign) to the
note of B-natural. When a melody in a major key is harmonized using only
the notes of that key, there is only one major chord to include a flatted seventh and that is on the fifth (or the dominant) degree of the scale. What
distinguishes barbershop harmony from simple diatonic (major and minor)
harmony is that these chords appear on many different degrees of the scale.
Seventh chords that appear on a degree other than the fifth are called "secondary dominants."

There is one secondary dominant chord that appears on the flatted sixth
degree of the scale that has the distinction of being known as "that barbershop chord." In the 1910 hit for Bert Williams, "Play That Barbershop

Chord," it is this chord that the piano player "Mr. Jefferson Lord" was asked to play (see Ex. 5).[10]

The song is in the key of C-major, but the chorus opens with a secondary dominant chord on the flatted sixth degree of the scale (A♭-seventh). A chord on the flatted-sixth degree is rarely found in European tonal music. The reason for this is that diatonic (major and minor) chords are constructed from alternate notes of the appropriate scale. Chords are constructed from the first note of the scale, the third, fifth and (in a four-note chord) the seventh. Chords can be constructed using any note of the scale as the first note. In the key of C-major therefore resulting chords may be C-major-seventh (C-E-G-B), or D-minor-seventh (D-F-A-C), or E-minor-seventh (E-G-B-D), and so on. The chord of A♭-seventh is constructed from three notes that are not in the scale of C-major. The root note of A♭ is not in the scale of C-major, neither is E♭, as this is the minor third in relation to C; the note of G♭ (notated as F♯ in the illustration) is not in the scale of C-major either. The only note in this chord that is in the scale of C-major is the note of C itself, and therefore this is the only note that does not require an accidental. As it is clear that this chord is not derived from European diatonic musical practice, it raises the question how this type of harmony developed.

The barbershop seventh may well have developed from the practice of "cracking up a chord." Dr. Laddie Melton recalled singing in a New Orleans schoolyard quartet around 1910. "It was typical, almost, for any three or four Negroes to get together and, they say, 'Let's crack up a chord! Let's hit a note!'"[11] The principle was that having established a note, a chord would then be formed around that note.

Sigmund Spaeth explained a similar practice in barbershop singing in his 1925 book of *Barber Shop Ballads*: "Barber shop harmonies are most commonly employed with the leading voice hanging on to one tone, while the other parts move around it. Every song actually ends on the key-note, or 'tonic,' which is as it should be in barber shop, but the other three voices have their choice of a variety of effects for prolonging the blissful agony."[12] The objective is to create harmonic variation. Sigmund Spaeth claimed, "No barber shop quartet in history has ever been guilty of landing right smack on a tonic chord and staying there for three, four, or five beats of the final harmony." [13] Instead, the lead and bass hold the tonic note, the tenor and baritone sing new notes to produce a different chord, before resolving back to the tonic.

In attempting to form such chords, it seems likely that various harmonic combinations were tried until a satisfactory chord formed. The editors of

Example 5: Lewis F. Muir and William Tracey, "Play That Barbershop Chord" (1910)

Slave Songs of the United States may have observed a similar practice in the 1860s. They noted that the slaves seemed "not infrequently to strike sounds that cannot be precisely represented by the gamut," with frequent "slides from one note to another, and turns and cadences not in articulated notes."[14]

In *Barber Shop Ballads and How to Sing Them* (1940), Sigmund Spaeth gave the fundamental barbershop endings. These were the simplest endings, in that only the tenor and baritone voice changed their notes. The principle behind the barbershop ending is to take the final melody note and harmonize this with a simple major triad. In its simplest form, the lead singer holds the tonic note of C; the bass singer sings C an octave below; the first tenor sings a third above the lead (E); and the baritone sings a fifth above the bass (G).[15] However, they do not remain on this chord (see Ex. 6).

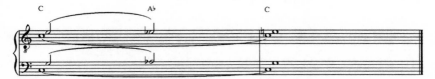

Example 6: Sigmund Spaeth's barbershop ending number 1 (*Barber Shop Ballads and How to Sing Them*, 1940)

This cadence is nominally in the key of C major—in that the first chord is a C major triad (C-E-G). The A♭-major chord is formed because the baritone voice that originally sang a G slides up to an A♭. Likewise the tenor voice that originally sang an E slides down to an E♭. This results in a barbershop chord on the flatted sixth degree of the scale, and forms "that" barbershop chord.

The second most fundamental barbershop ending that Spaeth gave is shown in Example 7. The tenor voice does as before and slides down to an E♭ (notated as its enharmonic equivalent D♯), while the baritone voice ascends beyond A♭ to A-natural. Notice that this tonic diminished chord is found (m. 8) in the chorus of "Play That Barbershop Chord."

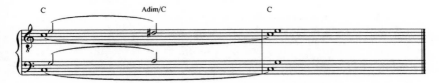

Example 7: Sigmund Spaeth's barbershop ending number 2 (*Barber Shop Ballads and How to Sing Them*, 1940)

The next most fundamental barbershop cadence, according to Spaeth, is formed when both the tenor and baritone voices slide up a semitone (see Ex. 8).

Example 8: Sigmund Spaeth's barbershop ending number 3 (*Barber Shop Ballads and How to Sing Them*, 1940)

A minor chord on the fourth degree of the scale (F minor) appears in (mm. 13–14) of "Play That Barbershop Chord"

If the tenor voice does as before and slides up a semitone, while the baritone slides up a tone, the result is a major chord (rather than minor, as in the previous example) on the fourth degree of the scale (see Ex. 9).

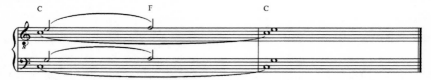

Example 9: Sigmund Spaeth's barbershop ending number 4 (*Barber Shop Ballads and How to Sing Them*, 1940)

This produces a cadence very similar to the plagal cadence in European music. Because of its association with church music, this is also known as the "Amen" cadence.

R. Emmet Kennedy and New Orleans Folklore

R. Emmet Kennedy was of Irish descent, but as a child lived in close daily contact with the local African American community. At the back of the house in Gretna was the New Hope Baptist Church. A woman who cooked and cleaned for his family, known to Kennedy as Aunt Julie Sparks, was a member of the church. Her two sons Sammy and Johnny were Emmet's childhood playmates and his next-door neighbors.

Kennedy recalled how as a child he would stand on a chair at the back of the house and try to sing along to the spirituals sung by the congregation. He learned musical notation and began to write down these songs. He wrote:

> In making the settings of these songs and spirituals it is my desire to give faithful transcriptions as my memory recorded the singing of the Negroes in my native town. . . . I have tried to follow as closely as I know how the intuitive harmonies and instinctive rhythmic peculiarities of these musical people, and have tried to suggest in the accompaniments the primitive, rudimental element so marked in all their productions.[16]

One secular song that Kennedy collected and reportedly performed in 1906 is "Honey Baby."

Roy Carew had befriended Jelly Roll Morton while he was in Washington in the late 1930s and accompanied him on at least one of his Library of Congress recording sessions. When the editor of the *Washington Post* ran an article saying that W. C. Handy was the father of the blues, Carew wrote a letter to the *Post*, titled "Birth of the Blues."

> For the sake of the record, I would like to say that the "blues" were known, played and sung in and about New Orleans years before Handy published his first blues number, "The Memphis Blues."
>
> For proof I refer to the book written by R. Emmet Kennedy, entitled "Mellows," published by A. & C. Boni. Among the songs in "Mellows" is one called "Honey Baby," a blues song. I know personally that Mr. Kennedy arranged this song and presented it in an entertainment several years before "The Memphis Blues" came out.
>
> Mr. Kennedy is a well known musician in New Orleans and vicinity and I have no doubt he remembers other blues numbers that were sung about the time he arranged "Honey Baby."[17]

Carew had known Kennedy in New Orleans and decided to contact him to find out when he had collected "Honey Baby." Carew wrote that in 1904, when he moved to New Orleans, he became acquainted with Kennedy, and that he heard "Honey Baby" performed by Kennedy and his niece who sang the song.

Some readers may remember the wordy battle between Jelly Roll and W. C. Handy in *Down Beat* in 1938 as to the origin of the blues. It seems that Handy permitted himself to be introduced over the air by "Believe It or Not," Ripley, as the originator of the blues, jazz and stomps, which naturally peeved Jelly Roll. As Handy's first blues, "The Memphis Blues" or "Mr. Crump" was not published until 1912, I was prompted to write to Mr. Kennedy and ask him when he arranged "Honey Baby." He replied to my letter from New York, where he had lived for many years, and he had the following to say about the song I heard in 1906: "Regarding 'Honey Baby,' included in my book *Mellows*, I feel certain that it goes back further than 1905. I had known it a long time before I arranged it for the piano . . ." So, from my personal knowledge, blues were known and played around New Orleans at least six years before the first blues number was published by Handy.[18]

In 1910 R. Emmet Kennedy had two books published in his Celtic name, Robard Emmet Ua Cinneidig. The first of these books was twelve Irish poems, *The Songs of Aengus*, that Kennedy had printed at Myers's printing House Ltd., New Orleans.[19] His second book of 1910, *Remnants of Noah's Ham (According to Genesis)*, was a "privately printed edition of two hundred and fifteen copies." The intention of this second book was to provide "Little sketches of negro life meant to show the better side of negro nature, in contra-distinction to the rough, belligerent side which is familiar to many that have seen the portrayals of the minstrel platform, and to many more who have listened to the modern 'coon song' melodies that have taken so strong a hold on the general public."[20] "Honey Baby," according to Kennedy:

was sung and whistled by Negroes of the East Green in Gretna and I got it in broken parts from Hattie Sparks, Michel Clay and a colored man called Cunjuh. By reconstructing the whole with the assistance of George Riley, who, though he denounced it as a "sinful ballet" and was not in sympathy with my interest in it, I was enabled to arrive at a version very close to the original through his memory of having heard it sung frequently on the streets and at meetings where "levity was free and in the ascendant."[21]

We know that Kennedy performed "Honey Baby" in May 1909 as part of a two-act play called *Dress Rehearsal*. The play was described as "A Laughable Nothing Done Into Music in Two Parts," by John T. Curlett and R. Emmet

Example 10: R. Emmet Kennedy, "Honey Baby" (*Mellows: A Chronicle of Unknown Singers*, 1925)

Kennedy. It contained a "Barytone [*sic*] Solo . . . Hello Central, Won't You Gimme Long Distan' Foam," in the first act.[22] Example 10 is the chorus with this lyric taken from "Honey Baby."

It is worth investigating further why Carew believed this was an arrangement of the first complete blues song he had heard. The "Hello Central" theme is found in a good number of blues and jazz songs, including Gus Cannon's "Poor Boy Long Way from Home,"[23] Jelly Roll Morton's "Doctor Jazz," and W. C. Handy's "Hesitating Blues" (1915). However, this alone is not the reason that this is a blues. An analysis of the melody and harmony shows that "Honey Baby" has the tonality of the blues.[24] The hallmark of a blues melody is that it contains both the major and the minor third. The major and minor third (E-natural and E♭) both appear in (m. 2); the minor third appears in (mm. 5, 6, 7) whereas (m. 8) contains the major third. Both E♭ and E-natural appear in (m. 10) and there is an E♭ in (m. 13).

Harmonically, this chorus begins on a chord on the fourth degree of the scale of C major. This "Amen" chord (F), corresponding to Spaeth's fourth most fundamental barbershop cadence, appears in (mm. 10, 13), as it does in Spaeth's fundamental barbershop cadences, with the note of C in the bass. In the second measure there is a note of E♭ in the melody. This is combined with a chromatic movement in the bass note from F-natural to F♯ and results in a chord of C-diminished (C-E♭-F♯). This chord is a version of Spaeth's second most fundamental cadence. In (m. 5) the appearance of the E♭ in the melody results in a chord of C-minor. In barbershop practice, this may result from the tenor voice descending from E-natural to E♭ while the other voices remain on their original note. In (m. 6) the appearance of the minor third results in augmented harmony on the dominant (fifth degree) of the scale. Spaeth notes: "One other fancy touch that appears frequently in barber shop harmony is 'augmentation' of an interval, which raises it by half a tone. . . . It occurs most commonly on the fifth, and again the confirmed barber shopper will recognize one of their favorite effects."[25]

Kennedy's transcription of "Honey Baby" clearly shows a close relationship between the tonality of the blues and barbershop harmony. His transcriptions also provide a unique record of the harmonic practices of African American singers in New Orleans around the turn of the twentieth century. He made it clear that he tried to accurately represent the harmonies of the singers that he transcribed, and in so doing presents compelling evidence that the tonality of the blues and the conventions of barbershop harmony were practiced in New Orleans at the time. This musical evidence is further supported by the recollections of early jazzmen.

Just as elsewhere, African Americans sang as they worked on the docks and on the levees of New Orleans. Steve Brown, a white bass player (b. ca. 1890), recalled:

> The ol' Negroes out there—I used to, many times, when I was a kid, go along the river and these Negro roustabouts would be sitting out on the cotton bales waiting for the boats, and they'd be singing. And they'd harmonize so beautifully, you know what I mean—oh, you've never heard anything like it in your life; I'd just be sitting around and listen at them for hours. And they'd just sing until the boat would begin to come to be loaded, and they'd have to go to work then. But

I'd sit around, and some of them would bring their instruments; and some of them would have a banjo or something, some of them would have a trumpet, an ole' battered up trumpet; and they'd play their tune, some, popular number, ah like they'd think it should be played, ya know—improvising and playin' it their way, their style."[26]

Jelly Roll Morton recalled singing in a barbershop quartet in his recordings for the Library of Congress: "Those days I belonged to a quartet. And we, of course, we specialized in spirituals for the purpose of finding somebody that was dead. And we could sing 'em too, I'm telling you. The minute we'd walk in—of course, we'd have our correct invitation—and that would be right to the kitchen where all the food was."[27] He then proceeds to sing "Steal Away" and "Nearer, My God, to Thee," demonstrating "some of the harmony we'd use. The boys had some beautiful harmony they sang. And, of course, we got together and made all kinds of crazy ideas of the harmony, which made it beautiful and made it impossible for anybody to jump in and sing."[28] Louis Armstrong also found wakes were a good opportunity to "eat and drink" to his "heart's delight." He remembered: "I used to go to a lot of wakes and lead off with a hymn. After everybody had joined in with the chorus I would tiptoe on into the kitchen and load up on crackers, cheese and coffee."[29]

The clarinetist Johnny Dodds and his brother Warren "Baby" Dodds (drums), who would work with Joe Oliver and Louis Armstrong in the 1920s, both sang in a family quartet. "Baby" Dodds remembered, "It was the most beautiful quartets you ever heard, to hear that outfit sing. I could sing soprano or tenor and my brother John used to sing real high tenor."[30]

Another New Orleans jazz musician to recall quartet singing from his teenage years was trumpeter Lee Collins: "There used to be lots of guys around New Orleans who could sing real good. They got up quartets—my Aunt Esther's husband was the head of many a one—and would go around to some of their friends' homes to sing and eat and drink beer. . . . That was some of the most beautiful singing you would ever hope to hear. After every one was drunk, the last song would always be their old favorite, 'Sweet Adeline.'"[31]

The guitarist Lemon Nash recalled a "barroom quartet" from around the time of World War I, in which Vic Little, "the best tenor singer in New Orleans," Al Whitney, and Monkey Joe sang. Among the songs were, "You Tell Me Your Dream" and "If You Could Fight Like You Could Love." Nash said that he accompanied them frequently.[32]

While there is ample evidence of quartet singing in New Orleans, until now there has been no direct evidence that Buddy Bolden may have been involved in barbershop singing. If he had been, and if he applied these practices with his playing, then this could explain how he introduced the tonality of the blues to the ragtime tunes he played.

Fred Ramsey interviewed Louis Jones, Bolden's barber friend, in 1954 for his research on Bolden. Jones told Ramsey that Buddy Bolden was the first man to play jazz and that he had just picked it up. He also said that at the time there were no other bands playing jazz. Ramsey questioned him on how he had picked it up if no one else was playing this kind of music at the time. Jones said he did not know. Edmund Wise (b. 1888) was also present at the interview. He had been responsible for taking Ramsey to meet with Jones. He told Ramsey:

> You see, in them days, there used to be quartets and all like that, you know. Well just like all them fellows would be singing, 'cause he had Cornish was playin' the trambone [*sic*] with him, he could sing, well they'd be singing around them bar rooms, well, just this was what they was singin'. . . . Mumford 'n them, well just what they was singing, Buddy Bolden going to play it. . . . Well if they'd sing it right, well, he'd learn how to play it right. . . . See, that's the parts he played it right.[33]

Wise remembered both Willy Cornish (Bolden's trombone player) and Brock Mumford (his guitarist) singing in this barroom quartet. It seems that Bolden had a very good musical ear. He could pick off notes as they sang. His ability to do this was confirmed by Louis Jones, who went on to say: "Buddy Bolden, I tell you what he would do—Buddy Bolden would take, and go to a theatre—or hear a band play somewhere, an' he come right back, and play it that night."[34] This is very clear testimony that confirms that Buddy Bolden sang in a quartet, had a good musical ear, and directly applied these practices to his instrument.

5

BILL RUSSELL'S AMERICAN MUSIC

A New Orleans "band of music" can be of any size and any instrumentation. Traditionally, the groups most favored have consisted of five to seven pieces with a more or less standard instrumentation. Each instrument has its own special role in building the final structure. Usually the trumpet (or cornet) is the musical, if not nominal, leader. He will call the tunes, except for requests; he stomps off the tempo to start the band; but mainly he plays or rather *sings* the melody (the "lead") in as beautiful and expressive manner as possible and helps drive the rhythm of the band. The trombone, big brother of the trumpet, also can sing a melody or a countermelody. Often he punches out a bass-like rhythmic part and utilizes the unique sliding (glissando) feature of the instrument. The clarinet, most expressive of all of the woodwind family, can sing voluptuously in the lower register or slash out dynamically in the upper register, but mostly the agile clarinet is used to "variate" and embellish the melodic line. Although all the "blowing instruments" of a New Orleans band are responsible for their share of the bouncy, pulsating drive, several other instruments [drums, bass viol, piano, and banjo] are specifically charged with supplying the steady fundamental beat of the band.[1]

In this discussion of New Orleans jazz, Bill Russell seems to have recognized that there was a strong relationship between the instruments of a New Orleans ensemble and song. As a trained musician and composer, Russell wanted to understand the principles that underpinned this music. Bunk Johnson, Bill Russell believed, offered a way to explore this relationship. Bill Russell wrote in *Jazz Quarterly* (Fall 1942):

Often when Bunk's band first announces the theme of a simple cho-
rale-like number, such as the spiritual "I Ain't Gonna Study War No
More," or "Storyville Blues," all the parts are played in a sort of pseudo
unison, or at least the parts are in similar rhythmic values. [. . . They
are] an ensemble whose unpredictable rhythms, vitalizing accents,
and independence of parts (even when playing isometrically) are more
thrilling than any symphonic group. There has been much talk about
New Orleans counterpoint, but the performance of Bunk's orchestra,
among others, suggest that possibly New Orleans ensemble style is
more of a heterophony than a polyphony.[2]

Bill Russell is said to have had "almost an obsession" with Bunk Johnson.[3] He never seems to have failed to respond to constant requests from
Bunk for money, even selling his own possessions on occasion. From his
modest resources, he set up and financed *American Music* principally to
record Bunk. Russell did record others, but within a few years of Bunk's
death his recording activity stopped completely. Why was Bill Russell so
obsessed with Bunk Johnson? Perhaps he knew something that few others
did and knew its significance. Bill Russell and Stephen W. Smith had written the "New Orleans Music" section of *Jazzmen* and therefore they had
a detailed knowledge of Charles Edward Smith's notes from the interview
with Willy Cornish in February 1939.[4] Therefore Russell knew—from the
best possible source—that Bunk Johnson had played with Buddy Bolden.[5]
Through his musical training, Russell knew that New Orleans jazz was un-
like conventional tonal music; it had a tonality that did not easily reveal its
principles through conventional analytical methods. Bunk Johnson was the
only known living link to the original Bolden band, and therefore he was a
unique source of both historical and, as importantly, musical information.
Bunk had not only played with Bolden, but was articulate, musically literate,
and possessed a remarkable memory. Through Bunk, Bill hoped, it might be
possible to understand the principles that underpinned jazz counterpoint
and the making of New Orleans style.

When Bunk Johnson was rediscovered, initial expectations about his
playing ability could not have been high. He was, according to his own esti-
mates, over sixty years old and had not played for some ten years. It seemed
too much to expect that he would be able to play with any authority. As it
turned out, he was still a very able musician. It is true that he was difficult
to work with, erratic in his playing, sometimes drunk or absent, critical of
the musicians around him, and capricious in his choice of material. Despite

this, Bill Russell, and others, recorded a remarkable series of interviews and performances.[6]

One difficulty was that Bill Russell and Bunk Johnson had two rather different agendas. Based on Bunk's claims (and Louis Armstrong's recollections), Bill Russell accepted that Bunk still "plays the old rags and marches exactly as he did in the 90's." That Bunk's playing had remained essentially the same was confirmed by Peter Bocage, who led the Superior Band that Bunk Johnson played in around 1908–10. He recalled that "Johnson played the same way in his youth as he did in later years, except for the effects of age."[7] Bill Russell wanted to record New Orleans jazz as it had been in the Bolden years, and Bunk Johnson was happy to oblige. However, this was principally because it might open the door to a little of the fame and fortune that his alleged onetime pupil Louis Armstrong enjoyed. His status as the old man of jazz was a means to an end, not an end in itself.

Louis Armstrong seems to have initially acknowledged the significant role that Bunk played in his own musical development. In September 1938, Louis Armstrong played a concert in New Iberia close to where Bunk lived. Bunk took the opportunity to attend and after the show spent some time talking with Louis, who gave him a photograph inscribed "Best Wishes To My Boy 'Bunk.' He's my musical insparation [sic] all my life—'yea man.'"[8] After initially enthusing to the *Jazzmen* authors about Bunk, and after a series of concerts where Bunk and Louis played together, Louis began to make it clear that it was Joe Oliver and not Bunk who had been his mentor. This was certainly true professionally. Joe Oliver was responsible for persuading Louis to leave New Orleans. In Chicago, Louis began a career that would spread New Orleans jazz around the world

Whatever Louis owed to Joe Oliver professionally, stylistically Armstrong and Oliver were quite different. Oliver preferred to play the lead melody and he used mutes extensively. Both Bunk and Louis excelled at playing second (harmony parts) with an open horn.[9] They had an easy, relaxed way of playing that was harmonically imaginative. The similarity of their playing was evident to New Orleans trumpeter Lee Collins (b. 1901). Commenting on Armstrong's first recorded solo "Chimes Blues" (1923), Collins said, "That sounds exactly like Bunk. You'd wonder sometimes if he was ever gonna get to the end of the phrase, or the chorus, in time, he's always so far behind, sometimes, but he always does . . . if you've heard that record you've heard Bunk."[10] This recording provides an interesting example of Armstrong's harmonic inventiveness. In a conventional twelve-bar blues in the key of C, the second bar would normally be harmonized with a chord of F-seventh.

Example 11: Louis Armstrong (solo chorus), "Chimes Blues" (1923). "Chimes Blues," by Joe King Oliver, copyright © 1923 (Renewed) by Louis Armstrong Music (ASCAP). All rights administered by Music Sales Corporation (ASCAP) international copyright secured. All rights reserved. Used by permission.

Instead, Armstrong, in his choruses substituted an Ab-seventh chord (see Ex. 11).[11]

In (m. 1) Armstrong plays the arpeggio of the chord C major. In (m. 2) the harmony moves to Ab-seventh. This is a secondary dominant on the flatted sixth degree of the scale. It is also an extension of Spaeth's number 1 barbershop ending and "that barbershop chord." In (m. 5) Armstrong introduces the notes of F and A while continuing to play C natural. This is Spaeth's number four ending and the "Amen" chord. The C-diminished chord (m. 6) of Louis's solo on "Chimes Blues" is an extension to the Ab-seventh that Louis employed in (m. 2). In fact, Armstrong only played three notes (C-Eb-Gb); another instrument provided the Ab. This is Spaeth's second most fundamental barbershop ending and the tonic diminished chord. Discussing (m. 6) of Armstrong's chorus, Gunther Schuller argues: "It is worth noting too that only in Armstrong's two choruses is the harmonic change made correctly. Louis moves up to an F sharp diminished chord [this is just an inversion of a C-diminished chord], where previously the ensemble had stubbornly tried an F minor chord, with pianist Lil Hardin blithely continuing in F *major*!"[12]

In the opening choruses of "Chimes Blues" the rhythm section plays a chord of F-major in (mm. 5–6). The following choruses of clarinet and piano chimes (m. 6) are harmonized with a chord of F-minor. As Schuller notes, this is not the result of any chord change on the piano; Lil Hardin continues to play an F major. It is the result of the descending clarinet line played by Johnny Dodds.

Example 12 demonstrates a combination barbershop cadence, or what Spaeth described as a "twice over" ending.[13] Because the clarinet is following

Example 12: Johnny Doddss chorus "Chimes Blues" (1923). "Chimes Blues," by Joe King Oliver, copyright © 1923 (Renewed) by Louis Armstrong Music (ASCAP). All rights administered by Music Sales Corporation (ASCAP) international copyright secured. All rights reserved. Used by permission.

the line taken by the baritone voice and plays an A-natural (Spaeth's number 4 ending), it can pass back through A♭ (passing through cadence number 3) before returning to G. It will be noted that the more fundamental (i.e., the lowest-numbered) cadences result from the smallest movement (or slide) in the tenor and baritone voices. The higher-numbered cadences result from larger changes in the baritone and tenor voices. As a consequence, if passing chords are used in combination to produce more elaborate endings, only certain combinations (progressions) are possible as the voices return back to their original note.

Louis Armstrong was familiar with the conventions of barbershop singing from a young age. He started singing in a quartet when he was around eleven years old. Armstrong recalled how he "started up a singing quartet with three of the best singing boys" from his neighborhood: "We used to hear the old timers sing around a bucket of beer—them beautiful chords—and we dug it. We was Little Mack, Big Nose Sidney, myself and Georgie Grey. Red Head Happy was in and out. . . . I was the tenor. I used to put my hand behind my ear, and move my mouth from side to side, and some beautiful tones would appear."[14] Armstrong tended to use the term "barroom quartet" rather than "barbershop." He further recalled: "I used to hear some of the finest music in the world listening to the barroom quartets, who hung around in the saloons with a cold can of beer in their hands, singing up a breeze while they passed the can around. . . . When I was a teenager, those old timers let me sing with them and carry the lead, bless their hearts."[15] He continued to sing in a quartet even after he was playing with bands. After the closure of Storyville red light district in 1917, he recalled, "My little crowd had begun to look forward to other kicks, like our jazz band, our quartet and other musical activities."[16]

Bunk and Bolden

On a Saturday afternoon in an upstairs room of Grunwald's Music Store in New Orleans, on June 13, 1942, Bill Russell had the opportunity to record Bunk Johnson talking about the way Buddy Bolden played. Bunk had earlier recorded three sides talking about his life, which were later issued on the *Jazz Man* label.[17] Russell still had one blank acetate disk left from an earlier session, and he didn't want to waste it. A few days earlier Bunk had whistled a tune that he said Buddy Bolden played, and Bill wanted Bunk to record this. Bill began by asking, "Well Bunk, you seem to be about the only one around here who remembers how King Bolden used to play. Can you tell us about what style of cornet he used to play?" Bunk agreed that he could give an idea of Bolden's style by whistling one of Buddy Bolden's tunes. He then began to whistle, unaccompanied, eight choruses of the tune that he claimed Buddy Bolden played. The tune had an eight-bar repeated structure where each chorus was a variant on the first chorus (see Ex. 13).[18]

Example 13: "Buddy Bolden's Make-up Tune"

In terms of form, the tune that Bunk whistled is consistent with later jazz, in that there is a single strain (or chorus) that is repeated with variations. There was, of course, no harmony on this recording. The chords are those implied by melody. In particular the A-diminished chord in (m. 7) could equally well be interpreted as an A-minor chord. However, Bunk does confirm that this is a diminished chord. Russell asked Bunk to tell him how he (Bunk) had introduced the diminished chord. Bunk said that he had played the same thing with Bolden and he would "make these breaks. I'd come in with diminished chords."[19] He then proceeds to whistle much the same tune for the first seven measures, and then in measure eight, Bunk whistled a series of A-diminished arpeggios (see Ex. 14).

The use of tonic diminished harmony is a feature of barbershop harmonization and the second most fundamental cadence in Spaeth's *Barber Shop Ballads and How to Sing Them.* Bunk Johnson claimed that he, rather than Bolden, employed these diminished breaks. But Bolden was familiar with barbershop harmonization; therefore it is reasonable to assume that both men employed this harmony (and this is implied by Bolden's melody as whistled by Bunk). But it may be that the figure itself was particular to Bunk. What this does demonstrate is that Bunk Johnson knew the significance of this type of harmony, which differentiated jazz from ragtime. Although diminished chords are used in conventional tonal music, it is very rare that the chord used will include the tonic note of the key. It is the tonic diminished (or one of its inversions) that harmonically stands in stark contrast to conventional tonal practice.

Example 14: "Buddy Bolden's Make-up Tune" (as Bunk played it with diminished chords)

"Careless Love"

It is clear from a number of Hogan Jazz Archive oral history transcripts that Bolden is credited with playing tunes that have been retrospectively called blues. A tune often cited as being a part of Bolden's repertoire is "Careless Love."

Howard Odum collected a number of versions of "Careless Love" for his 1911 paper in the *Journal of American Folklore.* Odum wrote:

There is abundant material for comparing with well-known folk-songs or ballads of other origins. One may note, for instance, the striking similarity between the mountain-song—

"She broke the heart of many poor fellows,
But she won't break this of mine"—

and the negro song "Kelly's Love," the chorus of which is,

"You broke de heart o' many a girl,
But you never will break dis heart o' mine."[20]

A version of "Careless Love" was also collected in Mississippi in 1909 from "country whites":[21]

I'm going to leave you now;
I'm going ten thousand miles.
If I go ten million more,
I'll come back to my sweetheart again.

Love, oh, love! 'tis careless love (twice)
You have broken the heart of many a poor boy,
But you will never break this heart of mine?

I cried last night when I come home (twice)
I cried last night and night before;
I'll cry to-night; then I'll cry no more.[22]

Despite most of the earliest folklore reports of "Careless Love" coming from white singers, there are also many reports from black New Orleans. Some New Orleans jazz musicians, such as Wooden Joe Nicholas (b. 1883, New Orleans), suggest that Bolden may have composed the song.[23] W. C. Handy claimed quite a different origin—saying the song "narrated the death of the son of a governor of Kentucky. It had the mythical 'hundred stanzas' and was widely current in the South, especially in Kentucky, a number of years ago."[24] This view does have some support: "In Henderson, Kentucky, the curbstone quartets improvised a song ['Careless Love'] about a local scandal involving a prominent citizen. The roustabouts and musicians carried it to New Orleans."[25]

Although "Careless Love" was performed in New Orleans, how well it was known in rural Louisiana is open to question. Some musicians from Louisiana say that the first time they heard it was in New Orleans.[26] John Joseph was born in Jamestown, St. James Parish, about eleven miles from Donaldsonville, Louisiana, around 1878. He says he began playing string bass around the age of eleven.[27] Bill Russell asked, "Did those bands up in the country ever play any blues at all?" Joseph said he "didn't know much about blues"; it was not until he came to New Orleans that he heard the blues.

> [Russell:] For a minute I want to ask about some of the old tunes, when you first heard them. Pieces like "Careless Love": when did you first hear that? When did you play it?
>
> [Joseph:] "Careless Love"? When I came down here, that was the first time I heard it. That's pretty old, too.
>
> [Russell:] When you first came to New Orleans, around 1906?
>
> [Joseph:] Around 1900, 1906, yes.[28]

The status of "Careless Love" as a blues has been the subject of some debate. Abbe Niles comments in *Blues: An Anthology* that "Careless Love," "despite loose references to it in *some books*, is obviously not a blues."[29] As he explained, "Many of the verses in the folklore are in the blues spirit, yet are excluded from the blues form. . . . In this usage, it was only the verses that could be fitted into the three-cornered tunes like *Joe Turner* that came to be called 'blues,' and, conversely, they would say of a new melody to which they could not sing one of their three-line verses: 'That ain't no blues!'"[30] His argument was that the only genuine blues were those that conformed to the twelve-bar form. The irony was that the composer and "Father of the Blues," W. C. Handy, included "Careless Love" in his *Blues: An Anthology*, and had invited his lawyer friend, Abbe Niles, to write the notes to the collection. For the lawyer it was easy to make the distinction between what was and was not a blues; for Handy, a musician, the distinction was less clear. It seems that Niles and Handy could not agree on this matter, even when writing in the same book.

Wooden Joe Nicholas heard Buddy Bolden play many times and liked "Bolden better than any cornet player in the world."[31] Unfortunately, we have no firm evidence of how Bolden and his band sounded, much less how they performed "Careless Love." Nicholas modeled his cornet playing style on Bolden and had firsthand knowledge of how Bolden played the tune.[32] It is for this reason that his recording of "Careless Love" is of particular interest.

On the recording, Nicholas plays a standard E♭ twelve-bar blues for the first three choruses. If Bolden performed "Careless Love" the same way, this alone could account for why the tune came to be considered a blues. However, there is another more fundamental reason why "Careless Love" is a blues: it has the *tonality* of the blues (See Ex. 15).[33]

Example 15: Wooden Joe Nicholas, "Careless Love," fourth chorus (*American Music*, MX803). "Careless Love" by W. C. Handy, *Blues: An Anthology*. W. C. Handy © 1926. Used by Permission of Handy Brothers Music.

According to Stephen Calt: "The building block of the blues is a four-bar phrase divided into two unbalanced parts: a ten beat vocal phrase, followed by a six-beat instrumental phrase. It is this unvarying phrase, repeated three times, that makes for a twelve-bar blues, and is the unique insignia of the form, removing it from the spiritual or any other song form."[34] As Calt notes, "Careless Love" used the "ten-six" phrase structure for its "first, second and concluding phrases."[35] What is unusual, as David Evans points out, is that in "Careless Love" the second phrase "ends on the major second of the scale, a characteristic rarely found in blues melodies."[36] This feature is evident in Wooden Joe Nicholas's version. He ends the second phrase on an F, the major second of the scale of E♭. Although rare in the blues, ending a phrase on the major second accompanied by dominant harmony is characteristic of tonal music and European folksong; this could argue for its Anglo-American origins.

However, the third phrase is rather more interesting. The melody of the third phrase in Nicholas's version of "Careless Love" ends on the minor third (G♭), whereas the first two phrases begin on the major third. The appearance of both major and minor thirds in a melody is, of course, typical of the blues. What is more, the minor third in this version of "Careless Love" is harmonized by a secondary dominant chord (B7) on the flatted sixth degree of the scale. These melodic and harmonic features are typical of early jazz blues and barbershop harmony but rarely encountered in other types of music.[37]

Bunk Johnson recorded "Careless Love" eleven times between 1943 and 1947, often at the request of Bill Russell.[38] The first of these recordings was made at the house of Bertha Gonsoulin at 1782 Sutter Street, San Francisco, on Monday, May 10, 1943.

Bill Russell was in San Francisco with Bunk Johnson for a series of lecture concerts that had been arranged by Rudi Blesh. Bunk often would not pick up his trumpet for months in New Iberia. To help "get Bunk's lip in shape" before the concert, Bill Russell arranged for Bunk to have what was "more or less . . . a practice session," with Bertha Gonsoulin on piano. Bertha Gonsoulin had studied piano with Jelly Roll Morton and she had played with King Oliver in 1922. She joined Oliver in California after Lil Hardin left the band and went back to Chicago.[39] Bill took his recording equipment along and recorded the session for his "pleasure and information."[40]

Bunk Johnson and Bertha Gonsoulin played their version of "Careless Love" in the key of F with no twelve-bar introductory chorus; they began with the sixteen-bar theme. In the opening chorus (m. 12), Bunk plays an F and Gonsoulin accompanies this with a D♭ chord on the flatted sixth degree of the scale. On the second chorus Bunk once again plays an F, but this time Gonsoulin plays a three-chord figure that cadenced back to the tonic chord (see Ex. 16).

Example 16: Bunk Johnson and Bertha Gonsoulin, "Careless Love." "Careless Love" by W. C. Handy, *Blues: An Anthology.* W. C. Handy © 1926. Used by Permission of Handy Brothers Music.

Using conventional tonal music theory, it would be difficult to explain how the cadence in (m. 12) functions. Particularly unusual (in terms of tonal harmony) is the D♭-major chord that contains its flatted fifth. The chords of European tonal harmony are derived taking alternate notes from either major or minor scales. Diatonic scales are constructed using either half steps (semitones) or whole steps (tones). As there are no scales that contain three consecutive semitones, it follows that the smallest possible interval in a chord is a minor third (a semitone and a tone). There are only two semitones between F and G, the major third and flatted fifth of D♭. However, in barbershop harmony a major chord on the flatted sixth degree of the scale that has a flatted fifth is quite common. According to Sigmund Spaeth, this is the fifth most fundamental barbershop cadence chord (see Ex. 17). In this cadence the tenor voice descends by a tone, and can therefore pass through E♭ (forming a simple A♭ chord) as it descends and ascends. This is a transposed version of the chords that Bertha Gonsoulin played in (m. 12, Ex. 16).

Example 17: Sigmund Spaeth's barbershop ending number 5 (*Barber Shop Ballads and How to Sing Them*, 1940)

"Make Me a Pallet on Your Floor"

Edward "Kid" Ory was born about thirty miles outside of New Orleans on Woodland sugar plantation in LaPlace on Christmas Day 1886.[41] At around the age of seven he made himself a banjo, a guitar, and a bass, and played with other local kids; they called themselves the Woodland Band. Before Ory made instruments for his band they were a "humming group." They would meet in a room sometimes, or often they would go out at night and sing on a local bridge. "In the dark, just couldn't see anyone, no one could see us, could hear us, you know, singing on the bridge."[42] Ory was asked, "what kind of tunes did you do when you had that humming group?" Ory said, "We hummed, and when we knowed the tune itself, the melody, one of us would take the melody, three-part, four-part harmony. . . . Sometimes we couldn't get the correct chord, you know, four-part harmony, we couldn't get it all the way through, we'd double up, you see."[43]

By around the age of ten, Ory had made enough money from playing fish fries to buy real instruments. His band at this time consisted of himself on valve trombone, Lawrence Duhé, Joe "Stonewall" Mathews, "Bull" White, Alfred Lewis on bass, and drummer Eddy Robertson.[44] One of the tunes that Ory recalled playing at the time was "Make Me a Pallet on the Floor."[45]

An early mention of the song can be found in a report from Pine Bluff, Arkansas, sent to the *Indianapolis Freeman* by the Dandy Dixie Minstrels in 1906. "The Texas Teaser, Bennie Jones sang 'Make Me a Pallet on Your Floor' with howling success."[46] The sixteen-bar melody is also found in 1908 in Blind Boone's "Southern Rag Medley no. 1." This was one of five *Strains from the Alleys* published by the Allen Music Company of Columbia, Missouri.[47]

W. C. Handy also made an arrangement of the tune around 1903 in Mississippi.[48] A further version of the song was reported by Howard Odum, sung by a visiting singer in Lafayette County, Northern Mississippi.[49]

Jelly Roll Morton recalled "Make Me a Pallet on the Floor" being played in New Orleans: "This one of, this was one of the early blues that was in New Orleans, I guess, many years before I was born. The title is 'Make Me a Pallet on the Floor.' A pallet is something that—you get some quilts—in other words, it's a bed that's made on a floor without any four posters on 'em."[50] Example 18 is Morton's version as sung for the Library of Congress recordings. This song has a number of features that are closely related to Emmet Kennedy's "Honey Baby." In both cases the opening chord of the chorus is on the IV chord, and in both cases tonic diminished harmony (or an inversion of it) is employed. This shows the clear imprint of African American quartet harmonization and also introduces the minor third to the harmony part.

Example 18: Jelly Roll Morton, "Make Me a Pallet on Your Floor." "Make Me a Pallet on Your Floor (Atlanta Blues)" by W. C. Handy, *Blues: An Anthology.* W. C. Handy © 1926. Used by Permission of Handy Brothers Music.

Bunk Johnson recorded "Make Me a Pallet on Your Floor" on four occasions. One of these versions is included in a "Bolden Medley" that he recorded with Bertha Gonsoulin. This medley also included "Bolden's Make-up Song" that Bunk had whistled for Bill Russell.[51]

After a four-measure introduction, Bunk introduces the theme by playing a variation on the "Make Me a Pallet on Your Floor" melody (see Ex. 19). Of particular interest is measure twelve: Bunk plays a minor third, whereas Morton sings the tonic at this point. Both of these notes will harmonize

Example 19: Bunk Johnson and Bertha Gonsoulin, "Make Me a Pallet on Your Floor." "Make Me a Pallet on Your Floor (Atlanta Blues)" by W. C. Handy, *Blues: An Anthology.* © 1926. Used by Permission of Handy Brothers Music.

correctly with tonic diminished harmony, but this does raise the question as to what extent Bunk was playing the melody. Arguably this is more of a harmony part. The same argument could also be made for Wooden Joe Nicholas's version of "Careless Love." When both Bunk and Nicholas imitated the way Bolden played, they played a harmonic variation on the melody.

Kid Ory didn't move permanently to New Orleans until 1908, but he did visit the city often before this time.[52] Bolden also performed in the countryside. Ory remembered that Buddy Bolden and his band would regularly pass through LaPlace and play from the baggage car of a train on the Yazoo and Mississippi Valley Railroad. The train would stop and the band would play to attract passengers for Baton Rouge. The band would play for an afternoon dance in Baton Rouge before returning to LaPlace around 8 p.m.

These visits appear to have influenced the repertoire of other bands. He recalled visiting bands led by Dave (possibly Henry) Peyton and Charlie Galloway. He said Peyton and Galloway played "mostly all Buddy Bolden tunes."[53] What is puzzling is that he claimed that at fish-fries (that he played at as a child) his band played "'Make Me a Pallet On the Floor,' 'I Think I Heard Buddy Bolden Say,' and quite a few more that I can't recall, you know, old numbers."[54] Taken at face value, what Ory is saying is that the Woodland Band, Charlie Galloway, and Peyton were all playing Bolden's repertoire before, or at much the same time as, Bolden became musically active.[55] It could perhaps be that songs such as "Pallet on the Floor," "Careless Love," and "Funky Butt" (the folksong that was associated with "I Thought I Heard Buddy Bolden Say") were in general circulation around the turn of the century. It could be that Peyton, Galloway, and Ory were playing these folksongs at this time, and that Bolden's contribution was to convert these folksongs into "the blues for dancing."[56]

Evidence for a pre-existing blues repertoire among New Orleans musicians, which Bolden subsequently applied to the instrumentation of a jazz band, comes from Louis Jones, Bolden's barber friend. He remembered an accordionist called Peyton, an older man than Buddy Bolden, playing "rag music" downtown before Bolden was playing. He remembered that Peyton played at the Custom House and Franklin in the Big Twenty-Five and also at the Little Twenty-Five on Poydras and Franklin. He describes the band as "something like a string band" with a "cornet player, bass fiddle, trombone and accordian [sic]."[57] Richard Allen asked, "Did Peyton play blues, at all?" Jones replied, "Yeah, he used to play blues too," but added that "he didn't become famous for his blues like Buddy Bolden did."[58]

John Joseph also remembered Peyton, saying he knew him well, and that he played a "wind-jammer" accordion, with buttons rather than keys, and that he would play the melody.[59] Willie Parker said that Peyton "could play the double row" accordion.[60] Eddie Dawson remembered an accordionist that he called "Lee Payton" who worked with a guitarist as a duo at the Big Twenty-Five who played a large accordion that "people called a 'flutetina.'"[61]

Eddie Dawson played guitar in Charlie Galloway's band for "two or three years." Galloway was a string bass player. He goes on to say that the older uptown bands, which included Galloway's, were called "ragtime" bands.[62] He says that Galloway worked "mostly in the country" along the route of the Southern Pacific and Texas and Pacific Railroads."[63] Galloway, he said, played a variety of music including "waltzes, schottisches, mazurkas, quadrilles, ragtime and blues."[64] It would be interesting to know when Eddie Dawson was playing with Galloway's band, as he goes on to say that the first time he heard a "band play the blues" was when he heard Buddy Bolden playing at Miss Betsy Cole's lawn in New Orleans.[65]

From this it seems possible that Galloway and Peyton may have played songs such as "Careless Love" and "Pallet on the Floor" at much the same time, or maybe before, Bolden. But these songs do not appear to have been known to those living on the Louisiana plantations. Most say that they first came to know these songs when they came to New Orleans, and exceptions like Kid Ory probably learned these songs from visiting New Orleans musicians.

"Mamie's Blues (2:19 Blues)"

Intriguingly, *Jazzmen* had stated, "Among the blues Buddy Bolden had to play every night were 'Careless Love Blues' and '219 Took My Babe Away.'"[66] This was potentially very significant. "The 219 Took My Babe Away" is an identifiable twelve-bar blues. If this came from a reliable informant, this would put beyond doubt that the blues in all its forms was performed by Bolden. Frustratingly, the authors do not indicate where they got this information. It is once again the interview that Charles Edward Smith conducted with Willy Cornish that solves the mystery. Cornish told Smith about the tunes he played with Bolden and said "two tunes you had to know: 'Careless Love Blues' and '219 Took My Babe Away.'"[67] This has profound implications. Jelly Roll Morton performed two versions of this blues (also known as "Mamie's Blues"); the first was for Alan Lomax at the Library of Congress in 1939. In both recordings he performed a twelve-bar blues with standard AAB stanza lyrics. If Morton's rendition of this blues is as performed by Bolden, then it is clear that not only was the tonality of the blues known to Bolden through tunes such as "Careless Love," but also the twelve-bar form was known to Bolden and his contemporaries. What is more, Cornish remembered this in February 1939, before Jelly Roll Morton recorded either of his versions of "Mamie's Blues (219 Blues)."

Jelly Roll Morton recalled that Mamie Desdunes lived next door to his godmother. "This is the first blues, I no doubt heard in my life. Mamie Desdunes, this was her favorite blues, she hardly could play anything else more, oh, but she really could play this number."[68] Morton gave further details:

Two middle fingers of her right hand had been cut off, so she played the blues with only three fingers on her right hand. She only knew this one tune and she played it all day long after she would first get up in the morning.

I stood on the corner, my feet was dripping wet,
I asked every man I met . . .
Can't give me a dollar, give me a lousy dime,
Just to feed that hungry man of mine . . .

Although I had heard them previously I guess it was Mamie first really sold me on the blues.[69]

From Jelly Roll's own chronology, we get further details about his god-mother. We learn that his mother died in 1899 and then he "lived with grandmother and godmother. . . . Godmother, Eulilie Echo [Haco][70] mar-ried Paul Echo, a cooper. Later she married Eddie Hunter."[71] But there is a problem in reconciling Morton's recollections. Mamie's address in 1900 is at 2328 Toledano.[72] Laura Hunter in 1901 and 1902 was living at the cor-ner house on 2706 South Robertson Street and 2621 Fourth Street.[73] They were several blocks apart. As Gushee notes, it was after 1901 that Morton "spent considerable time with his loving godmother, Laura Hunter/ Eu-lalie Hécaud, at one or another address in the black uptown ghetto of the tenth and eleventh wards."[74] Mamie was not a close neighbor at this time. It would be useful to confirm if these two women did at some time live next door to each other as Morton claimed; it would certainly help in dating this recollection.[75]

Another way to date this recollection is from the lyrics that Morton sang. When Morton recorded a commercial version of "Mamie's Blues," he sang:

Two nineteen, done took my babe away,
Two nineteen took my babe away,
Two seventeen will bring her back some day.[76]

Charles Edward Smith had been in the studio for the recording. He reported Morton as saying, "These were two fast trains; the first took the gals out on the T&P.R.R. (Texas and Pacific) to the sportin' houses on the Texas side of the circuit, Dallas, Texarkana, etc. The 217 on the S. P., through San Antonio and Houston brought them back to New Orleans."[77]

The 219 also appeared in Richard M. Jones's "Trouble in Mind." Jones was also from New Orleans. This adds weight to Morton's recollection that the train was associated with the city. Jones's version features the lines: "I'm gonna lay my head, on some lonesome railroad iron / Let that 219 train, babe, satisfy my mind."[78]

In January of 1901, Anthony F. Lucas struck oil in Beaumont, Texas. In the following decade, the population of Beaumont doubled as the Gulf Oil Corporation, the Texas Oil Company (Texaco), and Humble (Exxon) es-tablished pipelines and built refineries.[79] This rapidly changed the financial fortunes of the state. Under such circumstances, one can see why the pros-titutes of New Orleans would have travelled to Texas.

Bunk Johnson said he "knew Mamie Desdunes real well—played many a concert with her singing those same blues—good-looking—quite fair—nice head of hair—a hustlin' woman—a blues-singing poor gal—used to play a pretty passable piano around them dance halls on Perdido St.—When Hattie Rogers of Lulu White would put it out that Mamie was going to be singing at their place, the white men would turn out in bunches & them whores would clean up."[80]

Perry Bradford, a vaudevillian, composer, and arranger who would go on to write "Crazy Blues," which began the blues craze on phonograph records in the 1920s, may have also learned "Mamie's Blues" while in New Orleans. Speaking of his early career Bradford said:

> I joined Allen's New Orleans Minstrels in my home town, Atlanta, Georgia, in the fall of 1907. We played a two week stand in New Orleans at the fairgrounds during the Mardi Gras in 1908. . . . Every night some of our boys and girls would go slumming aroun' to all the saloons honky-tonks and dives, and to what the natives called the top-sporting houses, where no coloreds were allowed. This classy love-joint is where I first met Tony Jackson, whom the Creoles were acclaiming as the King piano man. But Tony was playing and singing songs that had drifted down from the north on down into New Orleans.[81]

Tony Jackson certainly had an extensive repertoire, and was recalled as the man "who knew a thousand songs."[82] Jelly Roll Morton considered him the "World's Greatest Single-Handed Entertainer. Playing all the classes of music in the style they was supposed to be played in, from blues to opera."[83]

Perry Bradford said that he left Allen's New Orleans Minstrels in Vinita, Oklahoma, and then went to Knoxville, Tennessee, and Chicago. This would have been after 1908 (according to his previous chronology). In Chicago, he entered a piano-playing contest. "I was short of money in Chicago and old 'Mojo' seemed to whisper in my ear, 'Sing and play your blues.' The first one I sang did it. I saw all the pimps with their gals and I remembered the verse of the blues that I started with."

> *My gal walked the streets in the rain and wet*
> *This is what she said to every man she met.*
> *I don't want your nickle [sic] just give me a lousy dime*
> *So I can feed this hungry pimp of mine.*[84]

This is the opening lyric that Morton used in his Library of Congress recording of "Mamie's Blues." According to Perry Bradford's recollection, he was

Example 20: Jelly Roll Morton, "Mamie's Blues (2:19 Blues)"

singing the same song after visiting New Orleans for the 1908 Mardi Gras. It seems likely, however, that Bradford may have dated this event somewhat later than it actually occurred.[85] From Lynn Abbott and Doug Seroff's research, we learn that Perry Bradford joined Allen's New Orleans Minstrels in the summer of 1903.[86] In addition, in a biography of Perry Bradford that appeared in the *Chicago Defender* in 1922, he arrived in Chicago in 1906.[87]

"Mamie's Blues" shows clearly the influence of barbershop harmonization (see Ex. 20).[88] The sheet music Morton published was in the key of F. The melody begins on the major third (A); in (m. 2) it is followed by the minor third (A♭) harmonized with a secondary dominant chord on the fourth degree in (mm. 5–6). In (m. 10) the minor third is harmonized with an augmented dominant chord—a practice common in barbershop harmony. The dominant chord in itself (C7) is not a fundamental barbershop chord; fundamental barbershop chords result from forming chords that contain the tonic note (in this case F). This could be an example of how the European perfect cadence became integrated into barbershop harmonic practice. The tenor voice in a barbershop cadence traditionally descends from the major third (A in this key) to the minor third (A♭). In melodic terms this is expressed as a blues third in (m. 10). Harmonically, it augments the dominant chord and results in C-augmented-seventh. This chord is not found in diatonic harmony because an augmented triad is formed from two consecutive major third intervals (C-E-G♯). A major third results from two consecutive whole-tones, and there is no diatonic scale that has four consecutive whole-tones.[89]

The recordings of Bunk Johnson, Jelly Roll Morton, and Wooden Joe Nicholas show clearly that the tonality of the blues was known to Buddy Bolden. This is not just confirmed historically; this is also confirmed by the music. In blues harmony there are specific chords that appear on specific degrees of a scale. These include secondary dominant chords on the flatted sixth and fourth degrees of the scale, minor seventh chords on the fourth degree of the scale, the tonic diminished chord, and the augmented dominant chord. All these chords contain the minor third of the scale. When these chords are sung or played in conjunction with the tonic major chord, cadences are produced that have both the major and minor third in the resulting harmony.

6

THE "CREOLES OF COLOR"

IT HAS LONG BEEN ASSUMED THAT DOWNTOWN CREOLE MUSICIANS
learned to play jazz from uptown musicians. While contact between musicians across Canal Street—the street that divides uptown and downtown New Orleans—was doubtless an important factor in spreading blues-inflected jazz, the availability of sheet music may also have been a significant factor for some Creoles. In 1908, Anthony Maggio published "I Got the Blues." In an article of around four hundred words titled "The Birth of the Blues," published in 1955 in the journal of Local 47 of the American Federation of Musicians, Anthony Maggio, a classically trained musician of Sicilian descent, claimed to have been responsible for the birth of the blues.[1] Maggio tells of a visit to Algiers on the opposite bank of the Mississippi to New Orleans in 1907: "I took the ferry boat from New Orleans across the Mississippi river to Algiers. On my way up the levee, I heard an elderly negro with a guitar playing three notes for a long time [see Ex. 21]. I didn't think anything with only three notes could have a title so to satisfy my curiosity I asked him what was the name of the piece. He replied, "I got the blues."[2]

Example 21: The melody that Maggio recalled hearing on a levee in 1907 (*Overture* 35, No. 9, 1955)

Quite why the elderly guitarist on the levee in Algiers chose to call the tune "I Got the Blues" we are not told. It may have just been a reference to his own state of mind, or it may have related in some way related to "I've Got De Blues" (1901), the first major hit for the African American vaudeville entertainers Chris Smith and Elmer Bowman.[3] Although this was not a blues in a musical sense, Jelly Roll Morton remembered, "The first publication with the title 'blues' as far as I can remember was a tune written by

Example 22: Anthony Maggio, "I Got the Blues" (1908)

Chris Smith."[4] Morton knew "I've Got De Blues," and it could therefore have been known elsewhere in New Orleans. Morton was wrong in his assertion that this was the first publication with "blues" in the title; however, none of the earlier songs had musical features that we normally associate with the blues. One of these earlier "blues" titles was "Oh Ain't I Got the Blues" (1871), performed by Welch, Hughes & White Minstrels.[5] An even earlier title is the 1850 comic ballad "I Have Got the Blues To Day," written by Miss Sarah M. Graham with music by Gustave Blessner and published by Firth Pond & Co. in New York.[6] The lyrics of all these songs make it clear that the concept of having the blues was identified in popular song with a depressed state of mind for more than half a century before Maggio heard a simple melody that inspired his 1908 composition.

Maggio goes on to say, "I went home. Having this on my mind, I wrote 'I Got the Blues,' making the three notes dominating most of the time" (see Ex. 22).

The same night [that he had been to Algiers] our five-piece orchestra played at the Fabaker restaurant (in New Orleans) 'I Got the Blues' which was composed with the purpose of a musical caricature, and to my astonishment became our most popular request number. In a very short time all of the negroes in New Orleans with street organs were playing the Blues.

During this time people asked me for copies, but I only had my manuscript. I had no intention of publishing it because my interest in music was entirely classical. However, the people's demand by now was so overwhelming that our first violinist, Barzin (later to play first viola with Toscanini at the Met) persisted until I finally consented to publish 1000 copies for piano, 500 for band and 500 for orchestra which were printed in Cincinatti [sic] by Zimmerman Publishing house. This took place in 1908. The copies were sold in a very short time. I wasn't interested in another edition for the reason already explained.[7]

Maggio reported that the elderly guitarist on the levee played a repeated three-note melody. There was nothing in this that suggests that his playing indicated any formal structure or any harmonic accompaniment. It is likely that Maggio chose to set this "musical caricature" in the twelve-bar form because he associated this form with African American musicians.

Maggio clearly was familiar with the tonal features of the blues. Of particular interest is (m. 6) of the twelve-bar strain. Chromatically altering the bass note of C to C♯ converts a secondary dominant chord of C-seventh (C, E, G, B♭) to a C♯-diminished-seventh (C♯, E, G, B♭). This is a diminished chord that contains the tonic note of G (the tonic), a characteristic of barbershop and blues harmony.

The New Orleans bandleader John Robichaux had an arrangement of "I Got the Blues" in his band library, but this was not the earliest twelve-bar tune in his collection. The earliest composition with a twelve-bar strain in Robichaux's collection is "Just because She Made Dem Goo-Goo Eyes" (1900), which the arranger J. W. Chattaway noted could be played as a "March or Two Step" (see Ex. 23). The eight bar introduction is followed by a repeated twelve-bar strain in E♭ using simple I-IV-V harmony. Robichaux's instrumental arrangement is arranged for piano, two violins, viola, bass, piccolo, clarinet in B♭, two cornets in B♭, trombone and drums.

"Just Because She Made Dem Goo-Goo Eyes" was a song "Successfully Introduced by George Primrose, in Primrose and Dockstader's Minstrels" in 1900, with music by Hughey [sic] Cannon and lyrics by John Queen.[8] The tune was extremely popular. A meeting of the Denver Federation of

Example 23: Hughie Cannon and John Queen, "Just Because She Made Dem Goo-Goo Eyes" (1900) (John Robichaux Collection, Hogan Jazz Archive)

Musicians "declared vigorously against ragtime," and cited "Ragtime Life" and "Goo-Goo Eyes" as two songs responsible for the craze that "has reached such proportions the prima donnas are now essaying it. Music teachers, in order to make a living, must shelve Clementi and Czerny, and teach the popular syncopation. Many performers' sole reputation depends on his ability to dispense it."[9] Another report of "Goo-Goo Eyes" comes from the *Daily Picayune* of January 9, 1902, where Billy Van performed the tune at the Crescent Theater, New Orleans. The song was popular with other early jazz musicians. Freddie Keppard, one of the early cornet "Kings" of New Orleans, played this tune.[10]

A second twelve-bar composition in Robichaux's library was "Since Bill Bailey Came Back Home" (1902). This composition, by Seymour Furth with words by Billy Johnson, was a reference to Hughie Cannon's "Bill Bailey, Won't You Please Come Home?" (1902). The verse of "Since Bill Bailey

Came Back Home" is a twenty-four bar strain in E♭, which is two twelve-bar strains repeated.

Of the titled "blues" to enter Robichaux's library, "The Memphis Blues" (1912) is of particular significance. Robichaux did not have a stock arrangement for W. C. Handy's earliest blues composition until 1914, but he did write his own manuscript arrangement. Robichaux is only known to have written special arrangements for twelve tunes. This suggests that Robichaux recognized how essential it was to have this piece in his band's repertoire.[11]

"The Memphis Blues"

William Christopher Handy was born November 16, 1873, in Florence, Alabama, the son of a Methodist pastor who was fiercely opposed to his son's interest in music. He reportedly claimed that he would rather see William "in a hearse" than hear that he had "become a musician."[12] Despite these warnings, William learned to play the guitar and later obtained a rotary valve cornet and took lessons secretly. After leaving school he worked as a teacher in Florence, but left in 1892 to take a teaching exam and a short-lived post in Birmingham. After the announcement of the World's Fair, Handy decided to make his way to Chicago with a vocal quartet and pursue his musical ambitions. When Handy discovered the World's Fair was postponed until the following year, he made his way to St. Louis where he found work at the Elliot Frog and Switch Works.

From St. Louis he went to Evansville, Indiana, and found work with a paving gang. He also contacted Phil Jones, a local brass-band leader in the area. One of the songs that Phil Jones sang was, according to Handy, a blues, "but the word formed no part of its title."[13] The song "Got No More Home Dan a Dog" (see Ex. 24) was later included in Handy's *Blues: An Anthology* (1926).

If the version in the anthology is an accurate reflection of the music that Phil Jones sang in Evansville in 1892, then it is highly significant as the earliest transcription (albeit notated retrospectively) of a blues performance. Not only did Handy record the lyrics, he also notated the melody and harmony. Perhaps most significant of all, he chose to notate this tune for a "quartette."[14] He does not say why he did this, but given that he was making his way to Chicago at the time with a vocal quartet, it is possible that this is how the song was performed.

Although the harmony is rather more complex in this arrangement than in a simple twelve-bar blues, it nevertheless follows the typical twelve-bar

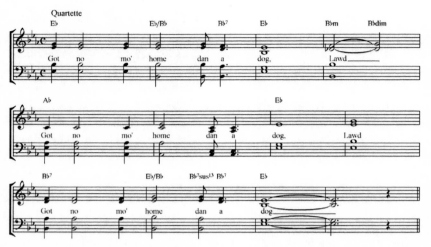

Example 24: W. C. Handy, "Got No More Home Dan a Dog," *Blues: An Anthology*. W. C. Handy © 1926. Used by Permission of Handy Brothers Music.

form. When Handy recorded a version of this song in 1938 for the Library of Congress, he accompanied his singing on a guitar with simple I-IV-V chords, thus demonstrating how easily this tune could be adapted for simpler harmony.[15] But despite the harmony and form of this tune being much the same as "The Memphis Blues," Handy claimed it was another experience that would lead him to write his first blues.

In the *New York Age* December 7, 1916, in the piece called "How I Came to Write 'Memphis Blues,'" Handy tells the story of hearing the song that would inspire "The Memphis Blues." "On a plantation in Mississippi I was awakened by a Negro singing a typical 'Blues' accompanying himself with a guitar tuned in the Spanish key and played in true Hawaiian style with a knife."[16] In 1941, with the publication of his autobiography, he would elaborate on this and claim that these events took place at a railroad station in Tutwiler, Mississippi.[17]

Whatever the significance of the guitarist in Mississippi, from a musicological point of view Handy's knowledge of quartet harmonization certainly influenced his blues compositions. He recalled that he had "struck upon the idea of using the dominant seventh" as the opening chord of the first strain of "The Memphis Blues" (1912). This he would claim, "was a distinct departure, but as it turned out, it touched the spot."[18] The opening chord for his first strain of "The Memphis Blues" is a dominant chord on the tonic note of the key (see Ex. 25). This would indeed be a departure from European

Example 25: W. C. Handy, "The Memphis Blues" (1912)

musical practice; but in barbershop harmony, dominant chords are the chords of choice. These chords are so fundamental to barbershop singing that the "barbershop seventh" has been described as the "meat 'n' taters" chord.[19]

"The Jogo Blues"

John Robichaux did not have a stock edition of W. C. Handy's "The Jogo Blues" (1913), but wrote part of it on the back of his "The Memphis Blues" manuscript. "The Jogo Blues" contains a very clear reference to the tune that would reappear with lyrics a year later as the "The St. Louis Blues" (1914). This is also the motif that Anthony Maggio recalled hearing on a levee in Algiers and which he used in his composition "I Got the Blues" (1908).

Also of interest is the harmony that Handy employed in "The Jogo Blues." Peter Muir claimed, "Probably the worst moment in the work" and "the weakest moment of any of Handy's blues—is the transition between the

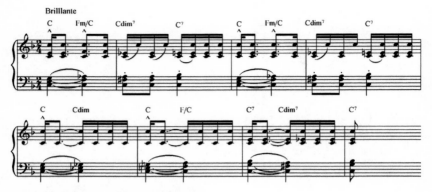

Example 26: W. C. Handy, "The Jogo Blues" (1913)

second and third strains. Melodically this consists of a single note . . . end-lessly repeated underneath an unchanging . . . harmonic pedal" (see Ex. 26).[20] In fact it is a masterful display of Handy's use of barbershop har-mony.[21] In these eight bars Handy uses all of the fundamental barbershop cadences—and what is more, they are arranged as they should be in a fun-damental barbershop cadence, with the bass and lead voice staying on the tonic note.

"The St. Louis Blues"

Robichaux had two published arrangements of "The St. Louis Blues" (1914): a 1927 reprint scored for B♭ instruments, which replaced an earlier edition, scored for transposing instruments. By the 1920s stock arrangements for cornets and clarinets were in standard B♭ pitch. This reflected the move away from the violin as the lead instrument in dance bands.

"The St. Louis Blues" is a composed blues, but Handy claimed it drew on elements of African American folksong that dated back to the late nine-teenth century. While in St. Louis around 1892, Handy fell on hard times. He later commented, "The misery of those days bore fruit in song."[22] While there, he heard a couple of "shabby guitarists picking out a tune called 'East St. Louis.' It had numerous one-line verses and they would sing it all night":[23] "I walked all the way from Old East St. Louis / And I didn't have but one po' measly dime."[24] He went on to say that "the tonality of these men's sing-ing may well have contributed to my writing of the 'St. Louis Blues,' but

Example 27: W. C. Handy, "The St. Louis Blues" (1914)

it should be clear by now that my blues are built around or suggested by, rather than constructed of, the snatches, phrases, cries and idioms such as I have illustrated."[25]

The first four measures of "The St. Louis Blues" provide an example of how Handy used barbershop cadences (see Ex. 27). Note the piano chord on the word "sun" and the sustained note of G in the bass. Handy provides an additional C in the bass, thereby converting an E diminished triad in the right hand to a chord of C-seventh—a secondary dominant chord on the fourth degree of the scale. Note also the augmented chord in (m. 10). This is the result of the minor third (B♭) in the melody augmenting the fifth of the chord.

The evidence of the sheet music suggests that, for at least some of the musically literate Creole musicians of New Orleans, the blues entered their repertoire through sheet music. Those, like Robichaux, who were able to write their own arrangements when published versions were not available had a considerable advantage. But there may also have been some Creole musicians who came to play jazz and the blues in a different way.

Alphonse Picou

Floraston Alphonse Picou was born October 19, 1878, and spent most of his early childhood living on Kerlerec Street, between Burgundy and Rampart Streets in the French Quarter of New Orleans.[26] His father, Alfred, was a "cigar maker"; his mother Clotilde was occupied with "housekeeping."[27] Around 1892 Clotilde was widowed.[28] At some point between 1893 and 1898, the family moved to North Robertson Street.[29]

As a downtown Creole, Alphonse had a conventional musical education. He also learned to play guitar from a paternal uncle, Autar Santami Picou, who was a poet. He gave conflicting accounts of his first clarinet lessons, saying variously that they were given by a flautist from the French Opera Company or from "Old Man Moret."[30] The latter was George "Na Na" Moret, a cornet player and leader of the Excelsior Brass Band, a downtown band "with reading musicians" founded in 1879 by Theogene Baquet and Sylvester Decker. When Baquet died in 1904, Moret took over leadership of the band.[31] According to William "Baba" Ridgley, "If you didn't know how to read, you couldn't play with Old Man Moret."[32] He had acquired his nickname "Na Na" because "he was very strict about band matters."[33] He was a musician who played "strictly from the music," but according to Hypolite Charles, who played with the Excelsior Band after WWI, "he couldn't play jazz."[34] He reputedly had "a beautiful strong tone, but he couldn't improvise or fake."[35]

When Alphonse Picou was around sixteen years old and practicing his lessons, he caught the attention of a neighbor who, according to Picou, invited him to rehearse with the downtown Independent Band—and by so doing introduced Picou to playing jazz. Picou claimed that the Independent Band did not use musical notation and played "by head." The significance of this, if this event did take place when Picou was sixteen, is that the downtown Independent Band would have been playing improvised music at a time when Bolden was only just beginning to take lessons on cornet from Manuel Hall, circa 1896. The widespread assumption has been that jazz first developed among uptown musicians and subsequently was adopted by the downtown Creole musicians. If Picou's recollections of the repertoire and methods of the Independent Band can be shown to be correct, this would rather suggest that jazz was developing in both uptown and downtown New Orleans at much the same time.

When Robert Goffin interviewed Picou, he was told that the young Alphonse had been interrupted from his clarinet exercises by a Creole who addressed him in French. The stranger announced that he was "Bouboule Augustin," and that, "this evening, I passed by chance in your street and I had my attention drawn by your style, easy and flowing with the clarinet." He explained that he had a free place in his orchestra. Alphonse asked, "Do you have the music?" Bouboule explained that they played "ragtime" that "normally, we play by heart."[36] In this interview Picou confirmed the information that he had given in the *Jazzmen* interview that he first played in Hopes Hall with the band, but to Goffin he dated this event to 1904. However, it is likely that Picou joined the Independent Band some years before this.[37] By 1904 Picou was twenty-six years of age; this is known because his birth certificate has been found.

In 1958 Bill Russell, Al Rose, and Ralph Collins interviewed Alphonse Picou. The Hogan Archive only has a summary of this interview, but Bill Russell kept a complete transcript. Picou told his interviewers:

> I was practicing on my instrument on my method, and him being right round the corner, Bouboul Fortunet, a little man, looked like a Mexican, he was a barber; now he had a band, and he needed a clarinet. So he came and knocked at my door. My mother went to the door. She says: "What can I do for you?" He says: "I like to know who's blowing that clarinet." She says, "That's my son."[38]

Picou was rather inconsistent in his recollections of the man who knocked on his door. He told Goffin that the man was the "conductor," rather than the trombonist of the band.[39] He also went on to list the band's personnel. "There was Bouboule Valentine (trombone), Constant (trumpet), Ascendor (bass), Richard Paine (guitar), Jean Vigne (Americanized as Ratty MacVean) (drums) and Valtout (violin)."[40] That in the same interview he should cite Bouboule Augustin as the "conductor" and Bouboule Valentine as the trombonist rather suggests that these are two separate people. The issue is further complicated by the fact that in 1944 and 1945, when Alphonse Picou (along with Sidney Bechet, Manuel Perez, Louis Nelson, and Willie Santiago) was interviewed by John Reid, Picou was asked: "Who were some of the men that played with you in the old Independent Band. On this occasion he identified 'Booboo Fortunet' as 'the manager and trombone player.'"[41] To further compound the confusion, Picou told Alan Lomax, when interviewed for *Mister Jelly Roll: The Fortunes of Jelly Roll Morton, New Orleans Creole and "Inventor of Jazz"*: "One day Bouboul Augustat, the trombone player, heard me practicing at the house and ask me if I want to come to one of the rehearsals."[42] And, this was "Bouboul's string band. . . . We had guitar, bass, trumpet, clarinet, and a songster."[43]

Whoever the visitor who overheard Alphonse Picou was, he was persuasive. His mother allowed Alphonse to come to his barber shop that evening at 8 p.m. It was only when he arrived that he discovered that this was a rehearsal of the Independent Band. The difficulty that Alphonse faced, despite this being a downtown band, was that they did not play from musical notation.

> The onliest thing I knew at that time was just notes. Nothing by head—notes. From my method. So, he says, "Come on. Tune up with us." So I tuned up with them. He said, "We're going to play a number— whatever you make, it's OK. On the clarinet." I said, "All right." I said "Lord," to myself. I said, "Now I'm in a terrible fix." So I sat down and, and with a good head, I got in with them.[44]

Alphonse impressed the band and they asked him to join them for a dance that they were playing that Thursday night at Hopes Hall on Liberty Street. Despite Picou's reluctance, he went to Hopes Hall. The place was packed and he "had to go up a stairway" to play. He remembered that they played "Chicken Reel," which he said he "knew that piece all right," and that while he was "blowing the life out of 'Chicken Reel'" the people were dancing.[45] They began playing at eight o'clock and finished playing at four in the morning.

If Picou did play "Chicken Reel" at this time, he could not have learned it from published sheet music; that appeared in 1910 subtitled the "Performer's Buck."[46] However, it is likely that the tune was in circulation earlier than this. A report from White City in the *Indianapolis Freeman* of September 28, 1907, noted a performer was "still singing 'Chicken' and doing his buck and wing turn."[47] "Chicken Reel" was also played by the bass player George "Pops" Foster (b. 1892), as a child.[48] He remembered how, with his older brother Willie (b. 1888), they would play for banquets on plantations.[49] George remembered that the bands they played in were "small, sometimes consisting of guitar, violin and bass, or mandolin, guitar and bass," and they "played old numbers like 'Chicken on a Reel.'"[50]

The day after playing at Hopes Hall, the band played for a picnic at Milneburg at Lucy's Pavilion. To get there Picou had to catch the 9 o'clock train from Elysian Fields and Claiborne. He continued to play out at Milneburg every week, and in so doing he learned how to play with "no music at all," and to "play head music, by ear."[51]

In *Jazzmen* Picou claimed that the "Independence Band improvised, rags, blues"; these included "The Blues" and "Careless Love Blues." When he was around 18 years of age, "they played loads of rags and blues, which he knew as early as he knew any kind of music."[52] If this is correct, and these events took place in the late 1890s, this is significant; it would indicate that at least one downtown Creole band was playing the blues at much the same time that this repertoire was beginning to influence the repertoire of the uptown bands. But this recollection seems to contradict another claim that Picou made. Sometime after he joined the Independent Band, Picou had a "little four piece band." One day the bass player Jimmy Brown and Alphonse Picou went down to the riverfront when railroad tracks were being laid.

At that time they was putting up the tracks; and they had one man that was singing the blues, you know?[53] I said "Jim, listen at that." . . . He was singing the blues. . . . He said, "Could you do something like that?" I said, "Sure." . . . I say, "Do you know the words of it?" "Oh," he say, "I've got that." So, I ran up my house, with him, I picked my clarinet up, and I blow that melody for him—that blues. And that night, we worked, because we (he) had a steady job, you know, and that night we put it on. That's where the blues come from.[54]

Picou gave a slightly different account of this to Alan Lomax.

I used to play on—in the night clubs at Villere and Iberville and they had a woman, a colored woman, working there, and she had a husband working on the railroad, putting up tracks, you know? And while working, he was singing, you know, these songs, and that's where the blues come from—the first blues. So she invite [*sic*] me and the bass player at her house. She says she's got a wonderful blues. She says, if we get that, it's going to be very good for the band. So the next morning we went to her house and I caught on to the melody and I wrote it down, from her, from her voice and, uh, with my instrument and I wrote the music down. And that night we came and we played it. [Laughs.] That was the first blues ever known.[55]

This cannot easily be reconciled with his recollection that the Independent Band played the blues at an earlier date. But it does seem to confirm that Picou is claiming to have converted a blues melody as sung by a railroad worker and adapted this to his clarinet. In so doing he specifically claimed that he was "the first man that composed the blues."[56]

Example 28: Porter Steele, "High Society" (1901), piccolo part transposed (Robert Recker arrangement)

Whether Picou first played the blues with the Independent Band or at this later time, he did not learn the blues either from an uptown band or through sheet music. Here we have convincing testimony that Picou, and the other musicians he associated with, directly engaged with converting songs into instrumental jazz. And this activity centered on the downtown barber shop of Bouboule Augustine at much the same time that Bolden was using Louis Jones's barber shop uptown as a base for his musical activities.

At a later date, however, Picou and his downtown associates did begin to work with uptown musicians. Picou later joined Peyton's "orchestra" with his old Independent bandmates Lily Ascendor on bass, Richard Paine on guitar, with himself as "the only improviser" on clarinet. Buddy Bolden, who had previously been with the band, by this time "flew on his own wings and monopolized success in the balls of Perdido."[57]

"High Society"

Alphonse Picou is particularly remembered for transforming Porter Steele's "High Society" (1901) from a march into a clarinet standard of the New Orleans repertoire. Picou took the piccolo solo from an arrangement by Robert Recker and adapted it to his instrument, and, in so doing, according to Sidney Bechet, it was 'put down in a fixed way.'"[58]

I have added the chords from the piano part to the same arrangement (see Ex. 28). It will be seen that the sheet music as performed by John Robichaux shows the clear imprint of barbershop harmony. The E♭ diminished chord in (m. 13) is an inversion of the tonic diminished chord found in Spaeth's barbershop cadences. Note also the barbershop chord of A♭ in (mm. 30 and 32). The secondary dominant chord on the second degree of the scale (D7) is also a barbershop cadence.

As is the case with all of Spaeth's fundamental cadences, only two voices (the tenor and baritone) change their note (see Ex. 29). As a consequence this is a three-note chord (D, A, and C) and in this instance this chord does not contain a third. The addition of an F-natural would result in a chord of D-minor-seventh; the addition of an F♯ would result in a chord of D-seventh (see Ex. 30). Spaeth also provided examples of endings in which three of the four parts move (but at most a tone and back again).[59]

It is interesting to compare these cadences with the way that Picou adapted his solo from the original piccolo part (see Ex. 31, with reference to Ex. 28 mm. 13–16).[60]

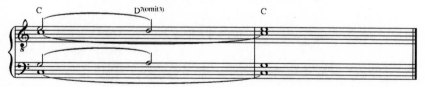

Example 29: Sigmund Spaeth's barbershop ending number 6 (*Barber Shop Ballads and How to Sing Them*, 1940)

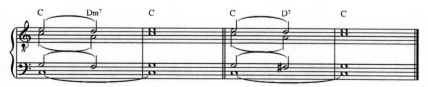

Example 30: Sigmund Spaeth's endings in which three of the four parts move (*Barber Shop Ballads and How to Sing Them*, 1940)

Example 31: Picou's adaptation of "High Society"

Although the rhythm section continued to play a chord of D-seventh, Picou played a D-minor-seventh arpeggio, exchanging the F♯s for F-naturals in (m. 14). This is consistent with one of the possible lines taken by a tenor voice in a barbershop cadence. In Spaeth's cadence (see Ex. 30), the baritone voice provides the third of the chord. Another possibility is for the tenor voice to provide the third by ascending from its start note of E-natural up a tone to F♯. To return to its original note, the tenor voice needs to pass through F-natural in (m. 14). There it can remain in (mm. 15–16) where it provides the flatted seventh of the G7 chord, before resolving back to E-natural in (m. 17) and a return to tonic harmony. Although a secondary dominant chord on the second degree of the scale is used in European tonal harmony—generally to effect a modulation to the dominant key—the voice leading is in the opposite direction. The F♯ usually applies upward chromatic tension on the root of the dominant chord. This is more consistent with the third being in the baritone voice, as in Spaeth's example.

By the turn of the century, the harmonic vocabulary of barbershop was beginning to appear among ragtime composers. This may in part explain why a tune such as "High Society" became a jazz standard. It also points to the complex processes involved in the making of jazz. Musicians may have directly applied the methods and principles of a barbershop quartet directly to their instruments; in other instances they may have been influenced by published sheet music, which increasingly used these harmonic formulations; and, of course, there is also the possibility of straightforward imitation.

7

THE ORIGINAL
DIXIELAND JAZZ BAND

WHEN THE ORIGINAL DIXIELAND JAZZ BAND (ODJB) RECORDED "THE Livery Stable Blues" on February 26, 1917, this was the first recording of a "jazz" band. The success of "The Livery Stable Blues" led to a copyright dispute. Chicago music publisher Roger Graham had produced the sheet music to "The Livery Stable Blues," but so had Leo Feist of New York, titled "The Barnyard Blues." Feist's edition had a front cover stating that it was identical with the "Livery Stable Blues," as recorded by the Original Dixieland Jazz Band.

Variety of October 19, 1917, reported on the court proceedings, noting that the case had caused much merriment and had been reported by the daily papers as "a comic feature story." However, despite the judicial "horseplay," this court case was of "considerable importance in the profession." In an effort to resolve the issue, an expert witness, a piano professor, "Slaps" White, was called. *Variety* reported:

> Professor White accomplished during his testimony what numberless others have failed to do. He defined "blues." The answer came when White told the judge he was the author of several hundred compositions, including several "blues."
>
> "Just what are blues?" asked Judge Carpenter.
>
> "Blues are blues, that's what blues are," replied the professor. The answer was written into the record and will stand as the statement of an expert.[1]

While this is hardly adequate as a musicological understanding of the blues, it does point to the difficulties that arise in trying to define the blues. It is telling, perhaps, that the court asked the opinion of an African

Example 32: Ray Lopez and Alcide Nunez, "The Livery Stable Blues" (1917)

American on the question. Dominick "Nick" LaRocca (b. 1889), the leader of the Original Dixieland Jazz Band, must have found this particularly irritating, as he always insisted that jazz had nothing to do with African Americans and that he and the white Original Dixieland Jazz Band were the originators of jazz.

What is verifiable about the origin of the "The Livery Stable Blues" is that LaRocca and Alcide "Yellow" Nunez (b. 1884) left New Orleans with Stein's Dixieland Jazz Band in 1916 and traveled to Chicago.[2] Nunez claimed to have co-authored "The Livery Stable Blues" with Ray Lopez (b. 1889), and they registered the melody for copyright.[3] Whoever was responsible for writing the tune, it is the manner of its performance that was particularly novel. This was a type of music in which a number of musicians were all apparently improvising at the same time. This nevertheless resulted in consistent harmonic form. Nick LaRocca described this as a kind of counterpoint that had its origin in song.

When he was young, Nick LaRocca worked as a stagehand at the French Opera House in New Orleans. As he explained, "I attended two arc lights on there and many of the ideas I got from listening to the songs they used to play—like playing counter-melody. Two songs at one time, which it became counterpoint, in my case. You listen to 'Livery Stable Blues'; you'll see what I mean. Take each instrument alone, and you got three melodies in there."[4] He expanded on this in another interview.

> The way we played was in fugue form. . . . I know nothin' about music, I'm just an ignorant scholar of music, but I went to many operas, opera places where I could hear good music, and I see how they played background contra-melody and different melodies against one another. I learned it at the French Opera when I worked down there handling lights when I was just a mere boy. I could see one person singing one tune and another one singing against it, whether it was contra-melody or not, but that impressed me much, and in later years when I incorporated that, what we had was nothing but conversation of instruments. You take "The Livery Stable Blues," for instance, I say to the clarinet da de da da da, Clarinet answer me, toodleeodetc. [sic] If you listen to them three of them distinct melodies. Take the trombone apart and you'll have a melody, take the clarinet, you'll have a melody, take the cornet, you'll have a melody, and they're three distinct melodies working together.[5]

An analysis of the melody and harmony of "The Livery Stable Blues" shows that the Original Dixieland Jazz Band was familiar with barbershop harmony (see example 32).[6] There is the alternate use of major and minor thirds in the melody and the consequent secondary dominant chord of F-seventh in (m. 5). This is then followed by a chord of F♯-diminished. The use of a diminished chord that included the tonic was the practice that Bunk Johnson claimed to have applied to "Buddy Bolden's Make-up Song." This harmonic feature was often found in the recording of uptown jazz, including in Louis Armstrong's "Chimes Blues" solo and in early blues sheet music, such as "I Got the Blues" (1908). The assumption has been that the Original Dixieland Jazz Band either copied these melodic and harmonic features from the black bands in New Orleans or they were familiar with these features from popular music of the period. But Nick LaRocca consistently denied this.

Nick LaRocca claimed that he played a blues similar to "The St. Louis Blues" before W. C. Handy published it in 1914. When LaRocca was

Example 33: A. J. Piron, "I Wish I Could Shimmy Like My Sister Kate" (1919) (Hogan Jazz Archive)

interviewed for the Hogan Jazz Archive in 1958, he claimed, "During 1912, '14, or '13 I played on the picture shows. I played on the J. S. excursion boat, I was hired there as extra man and I played the "St. Louis Blues," then known to me as 'Jogo Blues,' without the middle strain in it. And I played blues similar to that before I ever heard the 'St. Louis Blues'.[7] "The Jogo Blues" (1913) does indeed contain the strain that W. C. Handy would set to lyrics a year later in "The St. Louis Blues." It also appears in "I Got the Blues" (1908) by Anthony Maggio.

Both LaRocca and Maggio were Sicilian Americans, and it is possible that LaRocca may have heard "I Got the Blues." Maggio printed 1,000 copies of the piano score, 500 band arrangements, and a further 500 orchestral arrangements of "I Got the Blues"; these were sold by the Cable Piano Company on Canal Street.[8] We know that the leading Creole bandleader John Robichaux played the tune; it is possible that some of the white bands may also have done so. One white musician who was associated with Nick LaRocca was Ray Lopez, whose first experience of a dance band with a saxophonist occurred in the "Fabacher's Café."[9] This was the same restaurant to which Maggio had first introduced his "I Got the Blues."

It is tempting to dismiss LaRocca and the ODJB as plagiarists. We know from sheet music of the period, from Kennedy's folklore transcriptions, and from the recollections of the musicians themselves that this tonality was widespread. Black and white musicians often lived in close proximity. Harry Shields (b. 1899), the younger brother of the clarinetist with the ODJB Larry Shields (b. 1893), was born just two houses away from where Buddy Bolden lived.[10]

In fact, LaRocca did on occasion say that he played "Negro melodies."

> It's been said that we played many Negro melodies; that is true. . . . We had special arrangements on them; we used to get up—we didn't sing, but we used to holler, sing like we were—try to sing it. In other words, it pleased the public; they liked what we were doing, and they'd ask for the same thing over and we'd play them.
>
> [Allen:] Who did the singing in the band?
>
> [LaRocca:] Five of us—you know what I means?
>
> [Allen:] Yeah.
>
> [LaRocca:] I'd get up there and start "I Wish I Could Shimmy Like My Sister Kate" and so on. "Mama's Baby Boy." They were good numbers and we played 'em. The same as "Some of These Days," "Dark Town Strutter's Ball," or many other tunes that was owned by colored people we played. From that, all the people write about us. They said, "They played colored melodies." Sure, we played colored melodies. We also played melodies that were written by white people, but we didn't sing the white people's melodies. You'll ask me why. I don't know, because . . . they were made different."[11]

It is interesting that LaRocca recognized that melodies such as "I Wish I Could Shimmy Like My Sister Kate" were more suitable for singing as a group than was the case with tunes written by white songwriters. Who it was that actually wrote "Sister Kate" is disputed. Louis Armstrong claimed that he wrote the song, but it was Armand J. Piron, the New Orleans violinist and leader of the Peerless Orchestra, who received the copyright.

The underlying harmony of these opening bars of the chorus is a V-I cadence in E♭ (see Ex. 33). The opening chord of the chorus, D-diminished, is a chord of B♭-seven with the root of the chord (B♭) missing. The apparent harmonic complexity is a product of the voice leading. This is particularly apparent in the second measure; European chord symbols fail to adequately describe this harmony. One interpretation of the chord on the first beat of this measure is C-minor-sixth, although this is not entirely satisfactory from the standpoint of conventional music theory. The problem arises because in

Example 34: "Some of These Days"

conventional music theory, chords are constructed from the vertical stacking of thirds. If C is considered the root note of this chord (because it is in the bass) then we have a chord of C-minor-sixth (C-E♭-G-A). The difficulty is that G to A is not a third; it is only a second. The only way to construct this chord as a series of thirds is to place the A in the bass. This then results in a chord of A-minor-seventh-flatted-fifth (which technically is in first inversion because of the C in the bass). The appearance of the C-diminished-seventh chord a half a beat later does suggest an explanation for the apparent harmonic complexity. This is a tonic diminished chord that results from the voice leading (G-G♭-F) in the melody and the top note of the right hand piano chord. This voice leading is typical of the tenor voice in barbershop harmony, in which it is usual for the tenor to start on the major third (G in the key of E♭) and then descend to the minor third (G♭). Nick LaRocca seems to have recognized that African American songs were particularly suitable for collective singing, perhaps because of this melodic characteristic. "Some of These Days," another of LaRocca's favorites for collective singing, has the same feature (see Ex. 34).[12]

It could, of course, be argued that songs with melodies that contain both major and minor thirds would be particularly suitable for quartet harmonization because these melodies would be easily compatible with barbershop cadences. On the other hand there is some evidence to suggest that it is not the melody that gives rise to harmony in barbershop, but rather the harmony that changes the melody. Comment was made of the way barbershop singers would fit the melody to the harmony in one of the earliest references to "barbershop" singing. "Tom the Tattler," a critic for the African American *Indianapolis Freeman* (December 8, 1900), noted that for barbershop singers: "Their chief aim is to so twist and distort a melody that it can be expressed in so-called 'minors' and diminished chords. The melody is literally made to fit their small stock of slang-chords, instead of the chords being built around the melody."[13]

This line of argument is supported by a survey of the tunes that became barbershop favorites. Rather than complex melodies that contain unusual intervals, it is the simplest melodies that are favored. Songs that are particularly suitable for barbershop singing are based on the four notes of the Westminster Chimes of London's Big Ben (see Ex. 35).

Example 35: Westminster Chimes

Four of the most popular barbershop songs, including the "national anthem" of the barbershop movement, "Sweet Adeline," are based upon this simple four-note melody.[14] Other popular barbershop songs based on this four-note melody were "How Dry Am I," "And When I Die" (with the parody, "There Was a Goat"), and "Say Au Revoir but Not Good-bye."[15] The Westminster Chimes were also the basis of the piano chimes section of "King" Oliver's "Chimes Blues." The reason for the popularity of melodies based on these four notes, as Sigmund Spaeth wrote in his *Barber Shop Ballads and How to Sing Them,* was "that the harmonies all fall naturally into the forms of barber shop endings."[16]

Another group of tunes popular with barbershop singers are tunes based upon the pentatonic scale (see Ex. 36). As Rudi Blesh noted, "A very large number of work-songs, spirituals and blues melodies can be completely written in this scale transposed to the proper key."[17]

Example 36: Pentatonic Scale of C

The widespread use of pentatonic melodies in African American music was noted in 1872 by Theodore F. Seward. He transcribed twenty-three of the spirituals performed by the Fisk Jubilee Singers, and considered it "a coincidence worthy of note that more than half of the melodies in this collection are in the same scale as that in which Scottish music is written: that is, with the fourth and seventh tones omitted."[18] A survey "of *The Hampton Institute Spirituals,* which may be taken as representative, shows that spirituals with pentatonic melodies constitute about one-third of the total."[19] A similar ratio of pentatonic melodies was reported by the folklorist Henry Edward Krehbiel. In 1914 Krehbiel summarized the findings of his own and other song collectors' work in *Afro-American Folksong: A Study in Racial and National Music*. The book contains the analysis of 527 African American folksongs.[20] The largest single group of these folksongs used the major scale whereas the second largest group was pentatonic songs.

Ordinary major	331
Ordinary minor	62
Mixed and vague	23
Pentatonic	111
Major with flatted seventh	20
Major without seventh	78
Major without fourth	45
Minor with raised sixth	8
Minor without sixth	34
Minor with raised seventh (leading-tone)	19

There were very few songs that Krehbiel described as "mixed and vague," which rather suggests that very few melodies had both major and minor intervals. On the other hand, there is ample evidence that the practices of barbershop harmonization among African Americans (and others) were widespread by the late nineteenth century. If singers had confined their repertoire to those melodies that had both the major and minor thirds, they would have had a very limited repertoire.

There is clear evidence both from LaRocca's interviews (and also from the recordings of the ODJB) that LaRocca was familiar with African American vocal practice. LaRocca also claimed familiarity with the way that African American musicians played: "They'd start (doodleoddldoo) [*sic*] all together. Well, when they finished that one chord construction, with that tune, let me see 'em play another tune behind it. Well, I didn't do that. I coulda played the same way, but after I finished one tune in that same chord construction, they were all alike; they became all alike, there was no difference."[21]

Despite all the evidence to suggest that LaRocca and the ODJB were familiar with the playing of the uptown bands and were simply copying these bands, there is one thing in particular that suggests that this is not the case. According to Nick LaRocca:

> In my early training at school, at the closing exercise they had a number they called "The Holy City." Well I had learned this number and during the—Mr. Socolla was the man who taught us how to go

Example 37: Stephen Adams and Frederick E. Weatherly, "The Holy City" (1892)

through our little parts in the play—and the whole group was singing it. I was in the back singing, and I was making contra-melody on this tune, and he called me out the front and says I want you to sing this. And I got out there and I had stage fright, and I couldn't sing a thing, I couldn't remember what I did, but he thought I did something great that it would sound good if I would come out in the front and do it. Now that's, that chord construction is not from Africa. That is, the chord construction shortened is the chord construction of the blues.[22]

What LaRocca is saying is that "The Holy City" (see Ex. 37) has the eight-bar form of the blues rather than the twelve-bar form used in "The Livery Stable Blues" (see Ex. 32), and he discovered this by singing a countermelody as a schoolchild. LaRocca would later elaborate:

And we were singing "The Holy City"—[scats] "Hosanna" and so on— and I used to sing countermelodies against it. At that time I didn't know anything—I could show you on the piano how easy it is for me to get a melody, and many people say, "How you put them together?" Well, to me they come just like they come out of the air; all I need is

Example 38: Joe "King" Oliver, "Canal Street Blues" (1923), second strain. "Canal Street Blues," Words and Music by Joe Oliver, Copyright © 1926 UNIVERSAL MUSIC CORP. Copyright Renewed. All Rights Reserved. Reprinted with Permission of Hal Leonard Corporation.

four notes or five notes to start on and a chord construction to follow, and I can make a melody. And that's not only now; I've been doing this since I've been nine, ten years old.[23]

LaRocca is correct; "The Holy City" can easily be used as the basis of a blues. As David Sager noted in the sleeve notes to King Oliver, *Off the Record: The Complete 1923 Jazz Band Recordings,* the second strain of "Canal Street Blues" is "a paraphrasing of Stephen Adams' and Frederick E. Weatherly's 'The Holy City,' an 1892 sacred song hit" (see Ex. 38). This was not the only blues recorded by King Oliver in this recording session to make reference to "The Holy City"; "Chimes Blues" also quoted from the same tune (see Ex. 12).[24]

What Nick LaRocca seems to have described is the use of the same vocal harmonic principles in "The Holy City" that were employed by the uptown bands, and that gave rise to the distinctive harmony of jazz and the blues. LaRocca was certainly not the first person to employ this type of vocal harmony, nor the first to transfer these countermelodies to his instrument, but he does appear to be describing the same process.

Nor were the ODJB the only white musicians to recognize the connection between quartet vocal practice and jazz. George Brunies describes how he and other musicians, when they got together in the late 1950s, would "play on three way harmony," on trombones and trumpets. He went on to say, "They specialize in that harmony, that's pretty stuff. 'Course it's barbershop—a lot of those progressive guys call it corny or hicky, but that's what started music."[25]

"Papa" Jack Laine

Although Nick LaRocca may have learned some of his repertoire and developed the technique of playing countermelody independently, it is likely that much of the music that he and the ODJB recorded was already being played in New Orleans by Papa Jack Laine and his bands.

"Papa" Jack Laine was born in 1873, and he said he began playing drums around the age of eight "during the time of the exposition" in Audubon Park.[26] The World's Industrial and Cotton Exposition came to Audubon Park, New Orleans, in December 1884 and stayed until the following summer. Laine's first paid job was for a political parade when he was around fourteen years old. The tunes they played on this occasion were their own compositions. The band included Achille Baquet and Lawrence Veca. Achille Baquet was a light-skinned Creole and brother of George Baquet, who played with John Robichaux's orchestra. Due to his lighter skin, Achille worked exclusively with white bands. According to Laine, "all of the boys, these and the rest, would be whistling all kinds of funny stuff. When they got together, they would try to see if they could play that stuff over again." According to Laine, Achille "Baquet he's a wonderful man, he'd sit down, wonderful, boy, at least, he'd sit down in his shed, he had a shed, a woodshed, he'd get in that woodshed with his clarinet, and you have no idea the stuff he used to compose on that clarinet."[27] Laine said of "The Livery Stable Blues," "Achille Baquet and [Alcide] 'Yellow' Nunez composed it." He also said that the tune had different names and was also known as "Praline."[28]

By the time of the Spanish-American War, Jack Laine was leading his own band. He remembered that sometime later he took LaRocca into his band when LaRocca was just beginning "to make a scale" on his horn.[29] "I picked up LaRocca when had hardly [knowed?] anything about a trumpet [sic]. I'm playing the music on the street. Some fellow stepped [up]—it was told to me after—and wanted to know who was the leader of the band, they wanted to get a band to go to New York. LaRocca gave him a note; this fellow goes to LaRocca's house and sees LaRocca."[30] LaRocca then organized a band to go to New York without letting Jack Laine know. From this it is clear that "Papa" Jack Laine had grounds for a grudge, and his comments do need to be seen in this context.

Bill Russell interviewed Laine and asked him specifically, "Who wrote those old Dixieland pieces they call them today, like 'Clarinet Marmalade,' and 'Livery Stable Blues,' 'Tiger Rag.'" Laine said, "That's all our stuff."[31]

> Russell: Did you have the music for it or did you just make it up by ear?
>
> Laine: Made it up by ear, this man Baquet, that I'm telling you about is the man this boy right here that died recently, that boy, him and this man Vega and Manuel Mello they'd get together you know, cornet and clarinet, boy, they'd plan some stuff, make your hair stand on your head and go oh, boy, go as hard as the mischief with the crowd, throw the house down, throw the house down, yeah.[32]

Although "Papa" Jack Laine believed that Nick LaRocca learned all those tunes while playing in his bands, there were also some tunes that the ODJB played that were adapted from popular song.[33] Published in 1917, "Indiana," with words by Ballard MacDonald and music by James F. Hanley, would become one of the most enduring jazz standards (see Ex. 39).[34]

The Original Dixieland Jazz Band recorded "Indiana" on May 31, 1917, a little over a month after recording "The Livery Stable Blues." What is interesting is the harmony that is employed in this song. One interesting feature is "that barbershop chord" (E♭-seventh) in (m. 12). Another distinguishing feature is the use of diminished harmony. Although there are a good number of diminished chords in this composition, it doesn't necessarily follow that this indicates the presence of barbershop harmonization. It is only the tonic diminished chord that is particular to barbershop cadences. A case in point where diminished harmony is used is at the end of (m. 11). Here a chord of D♯-diminished-seventh (D♯-F♯-A-C) is used as an approach chord to E-minor. It will be noted that the tonic of the key (G) is not in this chord. This diminished chord applies chromatic tension to the E-minor chord; the D♯ is a semitone below the root of the following chord (E) and the F♯ applies chromatic tension to the third of the following chord (G). This is how diminished harmony is used in European tonal music; it is not how it functions in barbershop cadences.

It has long been accepted that the tonal nature of jazz is neither entirely African American nor entirely European. It has, however, not been easy to decide exactly how these traditions are related. One feature of ragtime and

Example 39: Ballard MacDonald and James F. Hanley, "Indiana" (1917)

jazz that has puzzled theorists is the dominant cycle of fifths. This is the chord sequence found in the first four measures of "Indiana" (G-E7-A7-D7-G). This chord sequence is very common as a turnaround at the end of a tune and can also be extended to form the basic harmonic structure of a tune. On the one hand, this chord sequence has features that appear European in origin; the root movement (the cycle of fifths) is typical of European

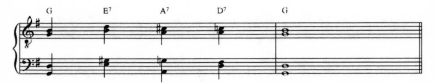

Example 40: Spaeth's barbershop cadence number 56

music. On the other hand, the consistent use of secondary dominants appears more typical of African American musical practice.[35] One way to explore this is to look at the voice leading of this cadence, since not only the chords themselves are different in barbershop harmony, the voice leading also is different.

Sigmund Spaeth did give a version of the dominant cycle of fifths cadence in *Barbershop Ballads and How to Sing Them*. In this cadence all voices move away from their original note (see Ex. 40).[36]

Where this cadence does appear consistent with basic barbershop principles is in the upper voices. After an initial leap of a minor third, the tenor and lead voice then return back in semitones to their original notes. However, the lower voices are less consistent with fundamental barbershop practices. The jumps of fourths and fifths in the bass voice and the leap of a tritone in the baritone voice are difficult to reconcile with barbershop practice. While it is possible to produce better theoretical models to demonstrate how barbershop singers may have developed this type of harmony, further research into how African American quartet singers and jazz musicians *did* voice these progressions would be rather more likely to shed light on the question. But this does demonstrate that an understanding of barbershop harmony, its voice leading, and principles, is a useful analytical tool in understanding the development of jazz and associated music.

8

$$\text{NEW ORLEANS}$$

Capital of Jazz

ROBERT GOFFIN VISITED NEW ORLEANS IN 1922 AND ON THAT OCCA-
sion met Bob Lyons, who had played bass with Buddy Bolden. On his return in 1944, Goffin decided to begin his research by finding Lyons. Lyons
told Goffin that he was born on September 16, 1870, in St. Jean Parish.[1] Bob
remembered that the first band that had a "notion of ragtime" was led by
Charlie Galloway, who played at Masonic Hall at the corner of Perdido.[2]
Galloway had a barber shop at the corner of Julian and Rampart Streets.[3]
It was here that Bob Lyons set up his shoeshine stand and the two men
became friends. Octave Landry played trombone in Galloway's band, and
Galloway wanted Octave's brother, Tom, to take up the bass. Instead, Tom
preferred to play the guitar. This gave Bob Lyons the opportunity to prac-
tice with the bass in Galloway's barber shop. Eventually he joined the band
that consisted of Octave Landry (trombone), Tom Landry (guitar), Charlie
Galloway (accordion), Willy Warner (clarinet), Frank Burnett (bass drum),
Edward Clam (snare drum), and a trumpeter who lived in Parish St. Jean.[4]

Bob Lyons told Goffin that he first met Buddy Bolden in Masonic Hall
around 1900 and that, at the time, Bolden played the accordion. Lyons was
playing with Charlie Galloway in Masonic Hall that evening, and Bolden
approached him to offer his services in the event that Galloway was sick and
unable to play. Bolden told Lyons that he lived with his mother and sister
at First Street and Liberty, and being unable to write, Lyons committed this
to memory.[5] Lyons estimated Bolden to be around eighteen years old at the
time. Given that we know Bolden was born in 1877, this would suggest that
this event probably occurred sometime before 1900. But the date of 1900 is
consistent with what a number of New Orleans musicians say; they do confirm that Bolden did not lead his own band until after the Robert Charles
Riot in 1900.

Bob Lyons stayed with Galloway for two or three years and, after discussion with Moustache, an Italian barman (and associate of Buddy Bolden), he joined the Eagle Band, which had been formed at the instigation of Moustache in the Eagle Saloon. By this time, according to Bob Lyons, Buddy Bolden had "changed instrument and achieved musical wonders" in an orchestra composed of "Bunk Johnson (trumpet), Frankie Dusen [*sic*] (trombone), Frank Lewis (clarinet), Brock Mumford (guitar), Henry Zeno (drums) and Bob Lyons (double bass)."[6] This is interesting because Lyons was interviewed by Charles Edward Smith and did not mention Bunk. In this interview with Goffin, Lyons seems to independently verify that Bunk played with Bolden and also to say that Bunk was still with Bolden after Willy Cornish had been replaced by Frankie Duson.

Goffin was confused by Lyons saying that Buddy Bolden didn't begin playing the cornet until around 1900; this seemed to contradict Bunk Johnson's claim in *Jazzmen* to have joined the Bolden band in 1895. His chance came to explore this further when he met up with "Big Eye" Louis Nelson Delisle.

"Big Eye" Louis Nelson was born in 1885 into a comfortable Creole family. His father ran a successful butcher shop and encouraged his son's interest in music. Louis took clarinet lessons with both Lorenzo and Louis Tio, who were considered among the finest clarinetists in New Orleans.[7] To try to establish when Bolden began playing, Goffin showed Louis Nelson a copy of Bunk Johnson's letter from *Jazzmen* that stated that Bunk Johnson had "left the Olivier orchestra to be hired by King Bolden in 1895." Nelson's answer was unequivocal: "This is not possible. Emmanuel Perez was the first trumpeter of jazz, around 1898, and Bunk came later!"[8] Nelson then took an extract from the *Times-Picayune* of July 1900 that announced the death of his father in the Robert Charles Riot. He went on to say: "This week, I played Club 28 with Buddy Bolden and he did not even have an orchestra of his own. He was a young apprentice who fingered the accordion and who played the trumpet for the first time" in a band led by Henry Peyton.[9]

Here we have testimony from two people who knew Bolden well, and who played with him, that Bolden began playing cornet around 1900. What is more, Goffin was given a very detailed account by Louis Nelson of where Bolden was, where he played, and who he played with, during the Robert Charles Riot.

On Sunday July 25, 1900, Robert Charles shot a police officer, and on the following Wednesday Charles was still at large. A large armed crowed began to rampage uptown and was heading toward the Club 28 where Nelson and

Bolden were playing. The band had been told that "blood ran," and Louis was concerned that his father was due to go out at midnight to collect his meat supplies for the following day. Louis wanted to go and warn his father not to go, but the other bandsmen persuaded him that it was not safe to leave.[10]

The police arrived at Club 28 and "a terrible brawl began." Several dancers were shot. Bolden, Jim Gibson (the banjo player), and Nelson hid behind the piano. During a lull in the fighting, the trio made their escape through a window in the gaming room that dropped down into an adjacent alley.[11] From there they managed to get into the back of Josie Arlington's. They climbed into the courtyard of Tom Anderson's Arlington Annex and, joining a number of others fleeing from the scene, ran along Basin Street. Eventually they found sanctuary in Louis Nelson's aunt's house at Orleans and Bourbon Street.[12]

The following morning the three returned to Club 28 to see what had happened to their instruments and other possessions. They had all fled without their coats, and Bolden was particularly concerned about the gold watch that was in his coat pocket.[13] The barman at the club was surprised to see them alive, and was also surprised that they had returned; the streets were still dangerous. There was "blood on the pavement"; police whistles could be heard, punctuated by what sounded like the "cries of animals" that had "their throats cut."[14] Bolden insisted on going into the ballroom. Victor, the barman, reluctantly led the way and opened the door. The curtains had not been opened, but, once their eyes had adjusted to the light, they could see thirty-five corpses laid out on the floor.[15]

The events of the Robert Charles Riot were etched on the memory of all in New Orleans who lived through it. It is unlikely that "Big Eye" Louis Nelson was mistaken about this, especially since Nelson was not alone in claiming that, at the time of the Robert Charles Riot, Bolden was not leading his own band. Bunk Johnson was asked by Goffin if he remembered when Buddy was "simply a musician" in the orchestra of Billy Peyton.[16] Johnson replied, "Buddy was with Billy Peyton and Big Eye Louis, at the time of the famous revolt when a Negro the name of Robert Charles killed a captain of the police force."[17] Alphonse Picou also said that, at the time of the riot, Bolden was still a novice. It is very unlikely that all four people are wrong on this. What, then, are we to make of Willy Cornish saying that he played with Bolden's original band before the Spanish-American War?[18] The balance of probability is that Bolden did not lead his own band until after the Robert Charles Riot; if Willy Cornish did play with Bolden at an earlier date, Bolden was not leading the band.

Leading the Band

At the turn of the century, the violin led a dance band. Emile Barnes (b. 1892) explained, "The violinist was the leader, because he played the lead [melody]; if there was no violin, the clarinet was supposed to play lead."[19] In interviews for the Hogan Jazz Archive the importance of the violin as lead instrument in a ragtime band is stressed by many of the early jazz musicians. John Joseph remembered, "Violin, oh, violin in the band, had them in [sic] the first and only instrument in those days, you know, before clarinet came out, was violin. That was the leading instrument, violin. . . . Yeah, they always took the lead; that was before they were using cornet, yeah."[20] Ed "Montudi" Garland (b. 1895) was asked "how a band worked when you had the violin lead. Then what did the clarinet play? What the clarinet would play if the violin played the lead. Would he play lead, too, or would he play variations or what?" Garland replied: "When the violin would play, play the melody, the clarinet playing harmony. Run crazy, run all around, you know."[21] Some violinists, such as Peter Bocage, may also have embellished the melody. He told his interviewers that the "violin part in ragtime is to play the lead, the melody, with improvisation."[22]

When there was no violin, or to produce variety, the convention was for the clarinetist to take the melody. The clarinetist in the Eagle Band was "Big Eye" Louis Nelson Delisle, who played C clarinet. This instrument was pitched so that it could play directly from a violin part. Wellman Braud (b. 1891) remembered that Delisle "used only C, played violin—played a violin part. Played lead sheet all the time."[23] Lawrence Duhé thought that "Big Eye Louis was the [best] clarinetist in New Orleans. He played lead, i.e., violin part as he used a C clarinet."[24] Peter Bocage said:

> the fellows we had in those days like Louis, he played a C clarinet, you see? . . . Well, he played off the clarinet part, see. . . . He would play—he would get the lead, and then he would make his own improvisations as he caught, you understand? . . . Yeah, his variation his own—his own ideas, you see. But, he would ah—after he would play it a while, he'd get the melody, you see, and he knew just how the tune went; and then, naturally, being gifted, in that type of playing, you know, he knew just what to put in there, you see.[25]

"Big Eye" Louis Nelson began to dedicate himself to the clarinet after losing his bass in the Robert Charles Riot. By 1904 he was working with a trio called the Ninth Ward Band. The band later increased to four members, with Johnny Gould (violin), Henry Ford (bass), Albert Mitchel (banjo), and himself on the clarinet. With this band he played "almost exclusively in the low register," and "it was a success!" It could be that in this band he did not play the lead and stayed in the lower register to avoid being in the same range as the melody that was played by Johnny Gould on violin.[26] Nelson was later hired by the Golden Rule Band, which played regularly at George Fewclothes' Cabaret on the corner of Liberty and Iberville.[27] Once again it was a violinist, Alcide Frank, who led the band.[28] To have played second to a violin lead, he would have needed a good ear and a good sense of harmony. These are qualities he possessed. According to Peter Bocage: "Well, for talent, he was very talented, you know what I mean; he was one of them fellows that could play most anything—if he heard it once, he could play it, you understand. And he knew chords—he was very gifted for that, and naturally that made him good, you see."[29] However, in the early years of the twentieth century the relationship between the instruments in a dance band was beginning to change. The fundamental change, as Louis Keppard remembered it, was that "'the clarinet, he's the one that takes the violin's place.' . . . It used to be that if there was no clarinet, the cornet took its place."[30] One of the first musicians to play lead on cornet was Manuel Perez.

According to Manuel Perez, ragtime began to be played by bands in 1898, and he associates this principally with the inclusion of drums in dance bands. Perez said that it was around this time that Louis Cottrell (b. 1875) began to play two drums at the same time.[31] This was revolutionary, because up to this time drums had been mainly used in brass bands. When they were used by brass bands it was necessary to employ both a bass drummer and a snare drummer. When early dance bands began to include drums, they also needed to employ two drummers. Bob Lyons remembered Galloway using two drummers. Who it was that first thought of connecting a foot-operated beater to a bass drum is disputed; a number of New Orleans musicians interviewed by Goffin credit this invention to Dee Dee Chandler. Louis Nelson thought that Jean Vignes should share the credit for introducing drumming to dance bands, and said that Dee Dee Chandler "did not start before 1900."[32]

This may explain one of the questions that has puzzled jazz researchers: why is Cornelius Tillman (the drummer) not in the photograph of the Bolden Band that Willy Cornish loaned to Charles Edward Smith? One possible explanation is that this is a very early picture of the band and dates from a time before Tillman joined the band. It is perhaps also telling that Cornish only mentioned one drummer in Bolden's original band, and not two as was the convention around the turn of the century.

The inclusion of drums in a dance band, according to Manuel Perez, had an important consequence: "it brought a revolutionary percussive power," and this led Perez to start playing ragtime on his cornet.[33] Around 1900, Perez started to lead his own Imperial Orchestra. By 1905, Louis Nelson had left the Golden Rule Band and joined Perez with Jimmy Palao (violin), Buddy Johnson (trombone), Jean Vignes (drums), and Bill Murray (bass).[34] This was unusual for the time: a dance band led by a cornet player rather than by Palao on violin.

Goffin asked Manuel Perez about the early years of ragtime and Buddy Bolden. He was told: "At this period, Buddy Bolden did not exist. He appeared only three or four years later. He was initially an accordionist. . . . We had little contact with his group" because Bolden came from "uptown."[35] According to Perez, in later years they did play opposite each other at Lincoln and Johnson Parks. At one time Buddy Bolden and Manuel Perez had a competition. They arranged to meet with their bands at Globe Hall, but Bolden did not appear. Bolden's friend Moustache explained that Bolden had been engaged to play elsewhere.[36] Alcide "Slow Drag" Pavageau (b. 1888) remembered the incident and believed that Bolden didn't turn up because "he was scared."[37] It is likely that this incident took place late in Bolden's playing career, because "Slow Drag" remembered that "'Big Eye' Louis was playing with Manuel" and at that time Frankie Duson "was playing trombone with Buddy Bolden," and Bob Lyons "was the bass player."[38]

Although Perez probably pioneered the role of the cornet as a lead instrument, and was probably leading his own band a few years before Bolden became a bandleader, Perez thought of himself as a ragtime player. The change of lead instrument from violin to cornet did not—in itself—make the distinction between ragtime and jazz. It is Buddy Bolden who is consistently remembered as the first man of jazz. The recollection of Peter Bocage is typical.

> Well, I attribute it to Bolden, you know; I mean, cause—the simple fact, the way that things come about—you see, Bolden was a fellow, he didn't know a note big as this house you understand what I mean; and whatever they played they caught [learned by hearing] or made up, you see? Say—they made their own music, and played it their own way, you understand? So that's the way jazz started, you understand?—just through the feeling of the man, you understand? Just his,

his improvision [*sic*], you see. And then the surroundings—the surroundings at that time was mostly people of—oh, you might say of fast type, you know—exciting, you understand? And those old blues and all that stuff, you know just came in there, you see. And eventually the jazz business started to going, you see.[39]

In a New Orleans band, the leader is the person who plays the lead melody. This raises a question; what was Bolden's role before he became a bandleader? We are told by "Big Eye" Louis Nelson that Bolden first played cornet in Henry Peyton's band sometime before the Robert Charles Riot. Nelson told Robert Goffin that his first professional engagement was at the Club 28 with Huey Rankin (bass), Henry Peyton (accordion), Jim Gibson (banjo), Charles McCurdy (clarinet), Buddy Bolden (cornet), and Octave Brown (trombone). He had been asked to deputize for one of the musicians, and he had hoped that he was there to deputize for McCurdy, but it turned out that he was instead offered the bass of Rankin.[40] There were no drums in this band. Given that Peyton was the bandleader, it is likely that he played the lead on accordion. It could also be that he shared this role with McCurdy; beginning in 1905, McCurdy would share the lead with the violinist Gilbert "Bab" Frank (b. 1875) in the Peerless Orchestra.[41]

One of the few reports we have of how Bolden played comes from Wallace Collins (b. 1858). Collins was a member of Charlie Galloway's orchestra from the mid-1890s.[42] According to Collins, "the violinist Tom Adams played the melody straight while Bolden 'ragged' it," by which he meant that he would "take one note and put two or three in it."[43] According to Willy Cornish: "We'd make 16th out of 8th notes. We ragged everything. . . . We'd change the time and intonation. . . . We used to cross three tunes at once."[44] This strongly suggests that Bolden was playing what has come to be known as "second" to a violin lead. As was the convention at the time, it was usual for the cornet to play a supporting harmonic role. What was perhaps more novel was that he apparently was improvising or "ragging" his part. It could even be that he continued to play this role when he led his own band. According to Bunk Johnson, when he went into Bolden's band the "leader" was "Dada Brooks, now he was a violin player in Buddy Bolden's band."[45] This is probably Dee Dee Brooks, who played in the Bloom Philharmonic Orchestra around 1903 alongside Armand Piron and Charlie Elgar.[46]

If Bolden did usually play a supporting harmonic role, this would explain why he had two clarinetists in his band. Emile Barnes was asked directly what two clarinetists would do in the same band, as the interviewer had

seen the picture of the Bolden band that shows Frank Lewis and Willy Warner both holding clarinets. Barnes said the use of two clarinets was not usual, and that "when there are two clarinets, one is supposed to play tenor sax,
the sax playing variations and the clarinet leading."[47] We know from Willy
Cornish that Frank Lewis usually played the B♭ clarinet and Willy Warner
played a C clarinet.[48] It is therefore likely that Warner's role was to play the
melody while Frank Lewis played a usual B♭ clarinet part. If this was the
case, then it follows that Bolden was not playing the lead and was likely to
have played a countermelody. In this role the cornet player was required to
play at a level that did not overpower the lead instrument. In such circumstances any cornet player who played lead, or who played a countermelody
in a prominent way, would be considered loud, and by all accounts Bolden
was a loud cornet player.

Accounts differ as to the extent to which Bolden and his band could read
and write music. According to Marquis, although Bolden's band was "not as
technically proficient as the Creoles, . . . most were readers, and Bolden and
Lewis, at least, could write music."[49] Manuel Manetta (who played all instruments and worked as a piano professor in Storyville) confirms, in an interview for *Life* magazine, that "Bolden could read; so could Frank Lewis."[50] It
may also be that Lewis gave lessons in playing clarinet. Willie Elias Humphrey (b. 1879) said that he "started playing clarinet at the age of twenty-
three" and that "Frank Lewis taught him," and lists Lewis among the "best
clarinet players in those days."[51] It would be surprising if Humphrey had
taken lessons from someone who could not read or write music; his father,
James Brown Humphrey (b. 1859), had pioneered the teaching of Louisiana
brass bands using notation.[52] Another member of Bolden's band who was
musically literate was Willy Cornish. He told Charles Edward Smith that his
first trombone was a Christmas present from a white man that he worked
for. "The boss sent him to Charlie Nazor, a German, to take lessons." He
went on an amateur job and was embarrassed because he was not able to
read his part, so he went back to Nazor for some more lessons. He "learned
to read both clefs, bass and treble."[53] His wife Bella (who married him in
1922) was adamant that, in the time she knew him, "he played by note; he
never played by ear." The transcript goes on to record that "he could fix
[arrange][54] music, too—you know, he'd take them chords, he could fix the
notes, you know, all on them chords and all—he could do that. Where you—
I guess he learned all that when he was learning."[55]

It seems likely that all of the other wind players in Bolden's band could
read music, at least well enough to learn new tunes from a score. We also

know from Louis Jones that Bolden had a good ear and could pick off melodies. This was confirmed by Goffin's informants, who reported that Bolden would regularly attend the St. Charles and Crescent theaters and was always present during minstrel shows. In the evenings that followed he would try to "reconstitute passages which he had heard in the theater."[56] We also know that he could pick off harmony parts as Willy Cornish and Brock Mumford sang in their barroom quartet. This skill would have been essential to him when he played with Henry Peyton. His role in this band was to provide harmonic support and to find countermelodies (a function to which his original instrument, the accordion, is well suited). It is this ability—to play second cornet—that is fundamental to New Orleans–style jazz.

Buddy Petit

Among the early cornet players, one name stands out for his ability to play second. Buddy Petit (real name Joseph Crawford, b. 1887) did not record, and consequently we have no firm evidence of how he played, but his contemporaries acclaim Petit "as the equal of Armstrong."[57] A good number of the musicians interviewed by the Hogan Archive remembered Petit. According to Peter Bocage, Petit was a "routine" player in that he played by routine rather than using written music, but he was "a good trumpet player."[58] He went on to say, "That's where jazz came from—from the routine men ya understand—the men that didn't know nothing about music. They just made up their own ideas."[59] Octave Crosby (b. 1898) said, "Buddy Petit was a good trumpet player; he had fast fingering," but didn't get very far away from the melody.[60] He also confirmed that Petit's band "used no music, except for an occasional lead-line for the trumpet player; Buddy wasn't much of a reader, but had a good ear."[61] Alfred Williams (b. 1900) said: "Buddy Petit played ragtime music. Ragtime was what they called it before they changed the name to jazz. It had the same beat. Petit played with Scott Joplin numbers. Buddy was not a reading musician, just a routine, trumpet player, but he was very good."[62] Charlie Love (b. 1885) said of Buddy Petit, "He was a very nice little trumpet player, played by ear, though, he never did read nothing much."[63] As it is clear that Petit was a poor reader of music and played by routine, the question is: how did musicians who played by ear develop these routines? One possible answer is provided by Louis Keppard.

Louis Keppard, who was active in the New Orleans brass band tradition before 1920, explained how one band member "would give us an idea, and we would memorize [sic] [i.e., harmonize] behind them. Of course, we could only do that because we could chord with one another. That's what made it sound good; we'd organize like a quartet, like about six or five or four mens. Bass, baritone and alto. Everybody got their own parts."[64]

One way to rehearse a band is to organize it in much the same way that vocal quartets rehearsed. These practices were witnessed by James Weldon Johnson and J. Rosamond Johnson in *The Books of American Negro Spirituals* (1925 and 1926).

In the days when such a thing as a white barber was unknown in the South, every barber shop had its quartet, and the men spent their leisure time playing on the guitar—not banjo, mind you—and "harmonizing." I have witnessed some of the hilarity and back-slapping when a new and particularly rich chord was discovered. There would be demands for its repetition, and cries of "Hold it! Hold it!" until it was firmly mastered. And well it was, for some of these chords were so new and strange for voices that, like Sullivan's *Lost Chord*, they would never have been found again except for the celerity with which they were recaptured. In this way was born the famous but much abused "barber-shop chord."[65]

Instead of chording together with voices, they could chord with instruments. And just as in a quartet, somebody has to sing or play the lead. If this lead is played by the first cornet, the role of the second cornet is to find a countermelody that would correspond to the alto or baritone part in a vocal quartet.

Kid Thomas Valentine (b. 1896) began playing trumpet in the Hall Family Band on Reserve Plantation, and by the mid-1920s led his own band.[66] He is reported as saying, in a summary of an interview, that he "usually played lead when he used two trumpets, but he would sometimes let the second trumpet player play lead. The best second trumpet player in New Orleans was Buddy Petit; he played second trumpet in all the brass bands." He also commented, "Playing second trumpet is hard to do; playing third trumpet is even harder."[67] Thomas liked to hear Buddy playing second parts, because "Petit excelled at making up second parts."[68] Ricard Alexis (b. 1896) made a similar observation.[69] It is said that "Buddy Petit liked to play second behind Alexis because he never made many high notes, but made 'such beautiful things' down in the staff. This is what 'made him great.' He liked Alexis to play lead so he could play variations behind him, when they played on the street."[70] According to Alexis, "Nobody today plays like Buddy, who played beautiful stuff down low. He hardly ever went above the staff."[71] New Orleans trumpeter Lee Collins thought that Petit played "just like Bunk," with "a great big tone, and a beautiful soul, and he played with ah, great drive, he didn't play many high notes, but he didn't need to make no high notes."[72] Bunk Johnson also excelled at playing second. To play second cornet required an ability to not overpower the lead. Peter Bocage remembered that Bunk was

> a nice, soft trumpet player, you know, he never was a blaster, you know. . . . And he had a very nice style, you know; he was—you see, in those days, we played mostly this—all that music was played in a slow tempo, you understand? . . . And look like he just had the right touch to play that type of music, you understand? It was a "slur" style, like you know—like "Frog Legs" and all those old numbers—Joplin music, you know? And Bunk was—look like he was just cut out to play that type of music.[73]

Bunk Johnson claimed that he taught Buddy Petit. He said Petit was working at a glass factory at the time and "he couldn't hold a horn."[74] Ricard Alexis agreed that Bunk Johnson "started Buddy Petit off." Buddy would sometimes sit in for Bunk at the Big Twenty-Five Club and he "got ideas from him."[75]

New Orleans trumpeter Punch Miller especially liked the way that Buddy Petit played, and gave a particularly detailed account of his playing. Punch Miller (real name Earnest Burden) said he was born in 1894, in Raceland, Louisiana.[76] In fact, he was probably born later than he said; when he registered for service in World War I, he said he was only sixteen or seventeen years old and adjusted his date of birth to get away from home.[77] Although he didn't settle in New Orleans until after the war, Miller did have contact with New Orleans musicians before this time.[78] Miller confirmed that Petit "didn't make high notes" and didn't play loud. He tended to feature slow tunes like "Bucket's Got a Hole in It." He also played "tough stuff" including "Maple Leaf Rag," "Panama Rag," and "High Society." Punch said that when Petit played "High Society" he would let the clarinet play the lead and he would play second (see Ex. 41). He demonstrated this by playing the

Example 41: "High Society" as Buddy Petit would have played it.

first few measures of melody of the last strain of "High Society" (shown in the upper stave).[79] Punch then demonstrated what Buddy Petit would have played (shown in the lower stave).

"High Society," as written, had a number of features that suggest the influence of blues tonality. The third measure of the final strain—as published—has both the major third (G) and the minor third (G♭, notated as F♯). There is an interesting embellishment of the published melody in (m. 4). At this point the harmony is the tonic chord of E♭; the melody note is B♭ (the fifth degree of the scale). The lead of the clarinet then descends through A-natural to arrive on A♭ at the beginning of (m. 5). The melody then ascends chromatically to arrive back at B♭ in (m. 6). A similar parallel chromatic movement takes place in Buddy Petit's cornet line. His line descends from the major third (G) of the E♭ chord through G♭ (the minor third) to arrive at F-natural (the fifth of the B♭-seven chord). This is then reversed and he arrives back at the G-natural in the middle of (m. 6). From there, Petit's line repeats the descending chromatic line taken by the clarinet a couple of measures earlier.[80]

The underlying harmony of measures four, five, and six of this strain of "High Society" are an example of a conventional perfect cadence. But the voice leading would be quite difficult to explain from the standpoint of classical counterpoint. Considered from the perspective of barbershop harmony, the baritone voice starts on the fifth of the tonic major chord, and the tenor voice starts on the third of the chord. If both voices descend down a tone (passing through the intervening semitone), they then need to return back to their original note to complete the cadence. The resulting cadence will momentarily pass through a tonic diminished chord. This feature is

Example 42: Punch Miller demonstrating the way that Buddy Petit would run diminished chords in B-flat

found at the end of (m. 4), where a note of G♭ and A-natural appear against an E♭ in the bass, producing a chord of E♭-diminished.

Punch then goes on to say: "Only thing I can say about him, he used to run a lot of augmented and diminished chords and things on his horn. He was—he was—he was famous for that. He'd be playing something and he'd make.—He'd be playing something in B-flat" (see Ex. 42).[81]

There is a striking similarity here with Bunk Johnson's recollection of introducing tonic diminished arpeggios to "Buddy Bolden's Make-up Song." Punch Miller is describing the same characteristic in Buddy Petit's playing. He would on another occasion agree with the banjo player Clarence "Little Dad" Vincent that Petit was the first trumpet player to start "running diminished chords," but neither Vincent nor Miller was of Bolden's generation and Punch Miller explicitly said that he never heard Bolden. [82]

On the Record

By the time that New Orleans jazz was recorded, the instrumentation of dance bands had changed considerably. This is evidenced in the recordings of the period and in sheet music. Toward the end of World War I, in dance band arrangements the leadership role had passed from the violin to cornet or trumpet. This change can be seen in the sheet music collection of John Robichaux. As the premier dance bandleader in New Orleans, Robichaux was compelled to change with the times and increasingly found that he needed to employ jazz musicians. In early 1918, Joe Oliver left New Orleans to work in Chicago. The Original Dixieland Jazz Band had made their first recording and would in a few years be followed into a recording studio by "Kid" Ory's band. Louis Armstrong had been working for Fate Marable on the Streckfus paddle steamers, and in a story that has been told many times, was finally persuaded to leave the Crescent City by Joe Oliver. Once in Chicago, "Little Louis," as he was known at the time, and Joe "King" Oliver created a sensation, with Armstrong playing second to Joe Oliver's lead. There was, however, some flexibility in the arrangement, as Louis Armstrong recalled: "You know what King Oliver said to me? 'You gotta play that lead sometimes. Play the melody, play the lead and learn.'"[83]

The importance of the lead was explained by the clarinetist Steve Angrum, who said that he didn't "take his horn down much in the street [. . . as the] the members do not know where they are in the tune unless they can hear the lead."[84] It is clear that early jazzmen used the melody as their point of reference. As Peter Bocage remembered, "The older men, if they knew a piece, they'd stick mostly to the melody; and put a little improvisation in, you know, but they'd never get out of the chord, see?" [85] It was essential for the lead player to stay close to the melody so that the other musicians could find suitable harmony parts, whereas the essential art of playing second was to find a countermelody that harmonized with the lead. The important contribution that Armstrong made in Joe Oliver's band was to perform the same role that Buddy Petit and Bunk Johnson both excelled at—playing second.

In 1923 "King" Oliver's Creole Jazz Band would record for Gennett Records. These recordings documented a style of jazz that was in the process of change. As Gunther Schuller noted:

> Since that year [1923] jazz has experienced a prodigious development in terms of instrumental virtuosity, dynamic and timbral variety. It is, therefore, all the more amazing that we can still listen with interest to the Creole Jazz Band, since these features are virtually nonexistent on its recordings. . . . The polyphonic density remains the same throughout each piece and each instrument remains in the prescribed range. . . . Each piece is like a solid, horizontally spun-out block of sound, maintained at an unswervingly steady pace and density. And yet we are fascinated because the linear and vertical details *within* this sound-block are, for the most part, continually varied in kaleidoscopic fashion. Occasionally the linear complexity borders on the chaotic; it may only be saved by the fact that all the lines are operating over a very simple harmonic structure. The accidental intertwining and crossing of instrumental lines makes out of these innocuous tunes and chord progressions a piquant listening experience, one that is enhanced precisely by the accidents of voice-leading that might easily be considered wrong in another (especially "classical") context: such as

the "wrong" notes, the chance parallelisms and convergence of lines, and their heterometric placement."[86]

The style of jazz played by Oliver's Creole Jazz Band may have already been a little dated; however, the extent to which these recordings were chaotic—in the sense that they were improvised in the moment—is open to question. As Lawrence Gushee noted, in the "King" Oliver recordings, "The impression of consistency is made all the stronger by the refusal of the musicians to permit themselves too much freedom. In successive choruses of a tune Oliver's sidemen often play the same part note for note, or with only slight variation—notice trombonist Honore Dutray [sic] in 'Froggie Moore,' especially; [Johnny] Dodds [clarinet] in the same tune and in 'Snake Rag.'"[87] The same is true of Armstrong's solo on "Chimes Blues," which almost certainly was not improvised. This was a rehearsed routine; Armstrong essentially repeated the same twelve-bar solo on his second chorus.[88] It is possible that the "Chimes Blues" solo may not have even originated with Armstrong. Some New Orleans musicians have claimed that this was played by Buddy Petit.[89] Within months of Armstrong's recording, Charlie Creath's Jazz-O-Maniacs recorded the same solo on "Market Street Blues," played by the trombonist Charlie Lawson.[90] While it is possible that he may have played the same solo because of Armstrong's recording, it is also possible that he may have come to know the solo from contact with New Orleans musicians. Creath's band worked on the riverboats and had the New Orleans drummer Zutty Singleton in the band for their recording of "Market Street Blues." Whichever is the case, it is clear that by this time this routine had become fixed.

According to Garry Giddins, one could "hear the future" of jazz in "Chimes Blues."[91] Early jazz bands did not play solos, but rather improvised collectively—or at least played routines that had been developed in improvised performance. Armstrong's solo on "Chimes Blues" in particular captures a moment when the transition to jazz as a soloist's music was taking place.

Armstrong, however, was not alone in pioneering the solo in jazz. From an account by Ernest Ansermet, a Swiss orchestral conductor who heard Will Marion Cook's Southern Syncopated Orchestra on tour in Europe, we learn that Sidney Bechet was performing clarinet solos in 1919.

There is in the orchestra an extraordinary clarinet virtuoso who, so it seems, is the first of his race to have composed perfectly formed blues on his clarinet. I've heard two of them which he had elaborated at great length, then played to his companions so that they are equally admirable for their richness of invention, force and accent, and daring in novelty and the unexpected. Already, they gave me the idea of a style, and their form was gripping, abrupt, harsh, with a brusque and pitiless ending like that of Bach's second *Brandenburg* Concerto. I wish to set down the name of the artist of genius; as for myself, I shall never forget it—it is Sidney Bechet.[92]

Bechet's ability was apparent from an early age. According to Peter Bocage, "He played everything—lead, counter-melodies, everything. Obbligatos—oh, he played anything that came to his mind, you see; he was just chock-full of music, full of ideas, you know. And he'd never get out of the key, though—that's one thing."[93] Bechet was also a keen harmonizer. He first came to know Louis Armstrong through his quartet singing and his association with Bunk Johnson. "It was Bunk Johnson who was the first to make me acquainted with Louis Armstrong. Bunk told me about this quartet Louis was singing in. 'Sidney,' he said, 'I want you to go hear a little quartet, how they sing and harmonize.' He knew I was crazy about singing harmony."[94]

An interesting example of the development of the solo in jazz is "Gut Bucket Blues" (1925). According to Johnny St. Cyr, Armstrong's Hot Five had only rehearsed three numbers for their recording session in Chicago, November 12, 1925. When they were asked to provide more, they decided to improvise a blues.[95] Johnny St. Cyr played a twelve-bar introduction. The band then played two twelve-bar choruses with all instruments playing in conventional New Orleans polyphonic style. The ensemble then proceeded to take twelve-bar solo choruses with Armstrong and Kid Ory introducing each of the soloists as they played. First Lil Hardin played a piano solo; this was followed by a solo from "Kid" Ory. Johnny Dodds took a twelve-bar chorus before Louis Armstrong paraphrased quite closely the solo that Ory played.[96]

Particularly interesting in Armstrong's solo on "Gut Bucket Blues" is that he chose to play three notes of C against a chord of G7 (see Ex. 43, m. 9). This should sound discordant, as the C should clash with the B in the chord.[97] If this was an isolated incident then perhaps this could be explained away as a mistake, but it is not. Armstrong played the tonic note where one would expect to find dominant harmony on other occasions; the same feature, for example, appears in "Mahogany Hall Stomp" (1928) and "Dipper Mouth Blues" (1936).[98] One possible explanation for this is that in a fundamental barbershop cadence, the tonic note is held by at least one

Example 43: Louis Armstrong's solo, "Gut Bucket Blues" (1925). "Gut Bucket Blues," by Louis Armstrong, Copyright © 1926 UNIVERSAL–MCA MUSIC PUBLISHING, A Division of UNIVERSAL STUDIOS, INC. Copyright Renewed. All Rights Reserved. Reprinted with Permission of Hal Leonard Corporation.

voice throughout. Rather than a mistake, a more credible explanation is that Armstrong knew exactly what he was doing. As he explained, "I had been singing for a number of years, and my instinct told me that an alto takes a part in a band same as a baritone or tenor in a quartet."[99] Armstrong was once asked whether singing in a quartet when he was young had affected the way he played. His response is telling. He replied, "I figure singing and playing is the same."[100]

9

THE BLUES AND NEW ORLEANS JAZZ

THE BLUES IN ITS RELATIONSHIP TO JAZZ HAS BEEN DESCRIBED BY Wynton Marsalis as "the roux in the gumbo," an essential ingredient in the authentic jazz mix.[1] In 1991 Paul Oliver raised some interesting questions about how the blues became a part of jazz.

> The role of ragtime, because the published compositions are specifi-
> cally datable, is less contentious, while the presence in New Orleans
> of known black brass marching bands in the 1880s and 1890s is well-
> documented. But what is the evidence of the presence of blues in New
> Orleans as an idiom distinct from jazz which could have exercised an
> influence upon it? Did New Orleans have a vocal blues tradition? If
> so, who were its exponents? If not, were its musicians first exposed to
> blues within the city (and if so, how?) or were they in contact with it
> while on tour, or in some other way? Were the New Orleans musicians
> the first to play blues-inflected jazz, or was it developed in another
> context altogether? The questions still remain. If there was any solid
> information on this subject it seems to have eluded most jazz histo-
> rians, though the recollections of various jazz musicians have been
> cited by some and must be similarly re-examined.[2]

This book is an attempt to answer these questions in both historical and musical terms. From a purely historical perspective, it is clear that the blues was performed in New Orleans in the early years of the twentieth century. Two specific titles were cited by Willy Cornish as having been played by Buddy Bolden, "The 2:19 Blues (Mamie's Blues)" and "Careless Love." It follows from this that Buddy Bolden played blues-inflected jazz rather than simply ragtime. The question that follows from this is how the blues became a part of the repertoire and tonality of jazz.

As Lynn Abbott has astutely observed, it was "the shared knowledge of the mechanics of quartet singing [that] apparently served the traditional brass band musicians of black New Orleans as a common point of departure."[3] Barbershop cadences give rise to specific harmonic progressions and particular voice leadings that are associated with the blues. It was through the application of these cadences and voice leadings to their instruments that the musicians of New Orleans developed New Orleans–style jazz. For musicians to be able to do this effectively, it would be necessary to have a good sense of pitch and harmony. The ability to read music would not be essential, but for reading musicians like Bunk Johnson it was not an impediment either. Having a good musical ear would have been particularly useful when performing folksongs. If there were no published arrangements of such songs, even reading musicians would be required to work out their own part, or create a written arrangement. This would perhaps not be too difficult for the lead instrument, which need only pick off the melody by ear; the real skill would be in inventing a countermelody to harmonize with the lead.

When countermelodies are played or sung using barber shop principles, these countermelodies inevitably will contain both major and minor thirds, as this alternation is fundamental to the tenor voice in barbershop cadences. This voice leading will also give rise to the distinctive chords associated with the blues and barbershop. If these countermelodies are played at a volume where they are heard as the lead, a blue-note melody will be the result. In so doing the most fundamental requirement of jazz will have been met; ragtime will have been spiced with the tonality of the blues.

This type of harmonization was sung in barber shops and bars, and by children on the streets. It was applied to popular songs and folksongs, both secular and religious. By the late 1890s, these harmonic features began to influence sheet music and published rags. There is also some evidence that Alphonse Picou and other Creole musicians were playing improvised rags and blues downtown using the same harmonic principles. It could even be that Nick LaRocca and the white musicians of New Orleans were also independently applying the principles of barbershop harmony to their instruments, and by so doing they could well have (wrongly) believed that they were the creators of jazz.

It has long been debated whether New Orleans is the sole birthplace of jazz. This is unlikely. We know from the recollections of W. C. Handy and others that the practice of quartet harmonization was widespread. We also know that brass bands flourished in cities and towns and also on rural plantations throughout the South. Given that musical literacy and pedagogy was not as developed in the rural areas as it was in New Orleans, the likelihood is that some rural musicians will have tried to play on their instruments the countermelodies they sang in quartets. There clearly is room for further research to establish if this was the case. But in such an environment, it seems doubtful that Buddy Bolden was literally the first person to apply these musical practices to an instrument. It seems likely that a good number of musicians would, at one time or another, have tried to play the kind of countermelodies that they sang.

There is at least some evidence of this in oral history transcripts with New Orleans musicians. It is clear that the early blues repertoire of songs such as "Make Me a Pallet on the Floor" and "Careless Love" were common to both Charlie Galloway's and Henry Peyton's bands. Although Peyton, as Kid Ory remembered it, played "mostly string music, . . . Galloway, he had horns." Given that Galloway had in the band at this time the trombonist Frankie Duson (who would go on to play with Buddy Bolden after Willy Cornish left the band), it is quite possible that Galloway's band was, as Kid Ory confirmed, "more like a jazz band," and possibly played a blues-inflected jazz some years before Bolden.[4] These early bands influenced Ory's own band at Woodland Plantation. Ory's band played a similar repertoire, and did so first on homemade and then on factory instruments, having graduated from singing in a "humming band."[5]

Although it is unlikely that Bolden was literally the first musician to play blues-inflected jazz, there is no reason to doubt what his contemporaries say: that he was the first musician to successfully exploit this practice before a wider audience. In so doing he become famous for playing "the blues for dancing."[6] Critical to broadening the appeal of this music was the opening of Lincoln and Johnson Parks in 1902. Lincoln Park provided a venue for Creole musicians such as John Robichaux, as well as uptown musicians such as Adam Oleavia. While there is no direct evidence that Bolden played at Lincoln Park, he did play in Johnson Park. The proximity of the two parks provided a point of interchange for both musicians and audiences. We know from the arrest reports of Masonic Hall that Creoles of Color did not venture in any number into this uptown venue, but they did go to Lincoln Park. In so doing, downtown Creoles would have heard Bolden in Johnson Park. For the downtown audience this was likely to have been the first time that they heard jazz. In this sense Buddy Bolden *was* the first man of jazz. Bolden was responsible for taking jazz beyond the confines of the uptown venues to a wider audience.

For many years the best firsthand evidence of the role of Buddy Bolden in the early years of New Orleans jazz has been treated with skepticism. Bunk Johnson tried to tell this story both in words and in music. For the most part, his testimony and his recordings have been discounted. It is absolutely clear both historically and musically that Bunk gave a very accurate account of the music of Buddy Bolden. Given that no recording exists of Bolden (and maybe never did), Bill Russell's recordings of Bunk provide the only musical evidence—from someone who actually played with him—as to how and what Bolden played.

Bunk Johnson's reputation has not fared well since the publication of *Jazzmen*, and it should be said that the reputation of the book itself has suffered as a consequence. But Bill Russell and Fred Ramsey never lost their faith in Johnson. The reason for that is now apparent. They both had access to the original interview notes, and they knew that it was Willy Cornish who had told Charles Edward Smith of Johnson's pioneering role in the making of New Orleans jazz.

NOTES

FOREWORD

1. Vic Hobson, "The Blues and the Uptown Brass Bands of New Orleans," in *Early Twentieth Century Brass Idioms*, ed. Howard T. Weiner, *Studies in Jazz, No. 58* (Lanham, MD: Scarecrow Press, 2009).

2. Vic Hobson, "New Orleans Jazz and the Blues," *Jazz Perspectives* 5, no. 1 (2011).

3. Vic Hobson, "Buddy Bolden's Blues," *The Jazz Archivist: A Newsletter of the William Ransom Hogan Jazz Archive XXI* (2008).

CHAPTER 1

1. There were also European collectors and jazz writers. See Hugues Panassié, *Hot Jazz: The Guide to Swing Music* (London, Toronto, Melbourne, and Sidney: Cassell, 1936); Charles Delaunay and Ian Munro Smyth, *Hot Discography* (Paris: Hot Jazz, 1936).

2. Pete Whelan, "Fred Ramsey Speaks Out," *78 Quarterly* 1, no. 4 (1988): 33.

3. Frederic Ramsey and Charles Edward Smith, *Jazzmen* (New York: Harcourt, 1939).

4. Harcourt Brace, "Press Release, February 19, 1947, Harcourt Brace, Box 11A," in MSS 559 (New Orleans: Williams Research Center, Historic New Orleans Collection).

5. The William Russell Jazz Collection and the Papers of Frederic Ramsey Jr. (New Orleans: Williams Research Center, Historic New Orleans Collection).

6. *Jazzmen* spelled his name Willy Cornish rather than Willie. I have followed the *Jazzmen* spelling.

7. Wilder Hobson, *American Jazz Music* (New York: W. W. Norton, 1939), 58.

8. Lynn Abbott, "'Play That Barber Shop Chord': A Case for the African-American Origin of Barbershop Harmony," *American Music* 10, no. 3 (1992).

9. Sigmund Spaeth, *Barber Shop Ballads: A Book of Close Harmony* (New York: Simon & Schuster, 1925); Sigmund Spaeth, *Barber Shop Ballads and How to Sing Them* (New York: Prentice Hall, 1940).

CHAPTER 2

1. Lynn Abbott, "Remembering Mr. E. Belfield Spriggins: First Man of Jazzology," *78 Quarterly* 1, no. 10: *78 Quarterly*, no. 10: 14.

2. *Ibid.*, 14.

3. "Jass and Jassism," *New Orleans Times-Picayune*, June 20, 1918; Bruce Boyd Raeburn, *New Orleans Style and the Writing of American Jazz History* (Michigan: University of Michigan Press, 2009), 19.

4. E. Belfield Spriggins, "Excavating Local Jazz," *Louisiana Weekly*, April 22, 1933; Abbott, "Remembering Mr. E. Belfield Spriggins," 14.

5. Willy Cornish, "*Jazzmen* Interviews, Box 16 C," in MSS 559 (New Orleans: Williams Research Center, Historic New Orleans Collection).

6. Frederic Ramsey Jr. and Charles Edward Smith, *Jazzmen* (London: Sedgwick & Jackson, 1939; reprint, 1958).

7. Al Rose and Edmond Souchon, *New Orleans Jazz: A Family Album*, 3rd ed. (Baton Rouge and London: Louisiana State University Press, 1984), 164.

8. Alden Ashforth, "The Bolden Photo—One More Time," *Annual Review of Jazz Studies* 3 (1985).

9. Typed notes from Charles Edward Smith interview with Willy Cornish, 2024 Perdido Street, New Orleans, La. 1939, Cornish, "*Jazzmen* Interviews, Box 16 C." The notes do not identify Smith as the interviewer but it is clear from "It's Tough—Trying to Run Down Jazz Facts" by Charles Edward Smith, *Down Beat* January 1, 1940 (Hogan Jazz Archive), that it was Smith who conducted this interview. There are also letters between Ramsey and Smith to corroborate this, "Box 21 A" in MSS 559 (New Orleans: Williams Research Center, Historic New Orleans Collection). Ashforth, "The Bolden Photo—One More Time."

10. In the *Jazz Archivist* (2009), Gerhard Kubik suggested that the photograph is a composite (a "photo montage") created from two negatives joined together. This is ingenious, but, as far as it is possible to be certain about anything relating to the Bolden photograph, it is incorrect. In the same issue Justin Winston and Clive Wilson suggested that the photographic process itself was responsible for the reversal of the images. Gerhard Kubik, "The Mystery of the Buddy Bolden Photograph," *The Jazz Archivist: A Newsletter of the William Ransom Hogan Jazz Archive* XXII (2009). I wrote a letter to the *Jazz Archivist* that appeared in 2010, to say that Willy Cornish's interview with Charles Edward Smith confirmed that the photographic process itself was responsible for the reversal. David Sager also wrote to say that Kubik had missed a crucial point about the construction of the valve-trombone and the cornet, and asked, "What is the likelihood of Bolden's cornet having been soldered together backwards?" Vic Hobson and David Sager, "Letters to the Editor," *The Jazz Archivist: A Newsletter of the William Ransom Hogan Jazz Archive* XXIII (2010).

11. The possibility that tintype technology may have created the reversal in the Bolden photograph was raised in Brian Wood, "Buddy Bolden and Billy the Kid," *New Orleans Music* 9, no. 5 (2001).

12. www.weneedtostop.com

13. Preston Jackson, "*Jazzmen* Interviews, Box 16 C," in MSS 559 (New Orleans: Williams Research Center, Historic New Orleans Collection); Ramsey and Smith, *Jazzmen*.

14. Rose and Souchon, *New Orleans Jazz: A Family Album*, 59. Other sources give 1902.

15. Louis Jones and Edmund Wise, "Interview Transcript, June 4, 1954, Box 9 B," in MSS 559 (New Orleans: Williams Research Center, Historic New Orleans Collection).

16. Louis Jones, "Interview Transcript, Jan 19, 1959," ed. William Russell Richard B. Allen (Tulane University, New Orleans: William Ransom Hogan Jazz Archive).

17. Jones and Wise, "Interview Transcript, June 4, 1954, Box 9 B."

18. Donald M. Marquis, *In Search of Buddy Bolden: First Man of Jazz* (Baton Rouge: Louisiana State University Press, 1978; reprint, 2007), 38.

19. Jones and Wise, "Interview Transcript, June 4, 1954, Box 9 B."

20. Robert Goffin interviewed Louis Jones in 1944 and reported: "Louis Jones knows that he was a barber but his testimony seems to relate to the status of workman rather than that of the owner." Robert Goffin, *La Nouvelle-Orléans Capital Du Jazz* (New York: Éditions De La Maison Française, 1946), 82.

21. Jackson, "*Jazzmen* Interviews, Box 16 C."

22. Jones and Wise, "Interview Transcript, June 4, 1954, Box 9 B." "Big Eye" Louis Nelson Delisle, Alphonse Picou, and Louis Jones all denied that Bolden had anything to do with the *Cricket*. Goffin, *La Nouvelle-Orléans Capital Du Jazz*, 82.

23. *Cricket*, Vol. 1 no. 1, New Orleans, March 21, 1896 (New Orleans Special Collections, Tulane University).

24. *Cricket*, Vol. 1 no. 8, New Orleans, July 24, 1897 (Xavier University); Kevin Herridge, "T'was in 'the Cricket' It Must Be So," *New Orleans Music* 9, no. 6 (2001): 16.

25. Goffin, *La Nouvelle-Orléans Capital Du Jazz*, 99. I have only been able to identify one Otis Watts who lived in New Orleans during this period. Soards' New Orleans City Directory of 1891 lists a laborer named Otis Watts at 311 Louisiana Avenue. The Parish of Orleans Federal Census of 1880 lists an eight-year- old Otis Watts (black) at home with his parents Henry and Pricilla at 486 Chippewa Street. The 1910 census gives him as born about 1872, mulatto, married and working as a porter.

26. It has been suggested that Manuel Manetta had copies of the *Cricket*, which he gave to Bill Russell. They are not in the Bill Russell collection at the Historic New Orleans Collection.

27. Richard M. Jones, "*Jazzmen* Interviews, Box 16 C," in MSS 559 (New Orleans: Williams Research Center, Historic New Orleans Collection).

28. Marquis, *In Search of Buddy Bolden*, 126.

29. *New Orleans Times-Picayune*, September 4, 1906.

30. Charles Edward Smith, "The Bolden Cylinder," *Saturday Review* December (1957): 35.

31. Charles Edward Smith, "Letter to Bill Russell, April 16, 1939, Box 21A," in MSS 559 (New Orleans: Williams Research Center, Historic New Orleans Collection).

32. Charles Edward Smith, "Letter to Bill Russell, July 14, 1939, Box 21 A," in MSS 559 (New Orleans: Williams Research Center, Historic New Orleans Collection).

33. Frederic Ramsey Jr., "Meeting Notes with Tom Bethel Sunday March 2, 1975, Box 10A," in MSS 559 (New Orleans: Williams Research Center, Historic New Orleans Collection).

34. Brian Woolley as quoted by Ray Coleman, "*Melody Maker*, March 9, 1963, Box 20 B," in MSS 559 (New Orleans: Williams Research Center, Historic New Orleans Collection). In the article, each of these sentences is a single paragraph.

35. Paige Van Vorst, "Jazz Expert Discovers Bolden Band Proof," March 1974, in "Charles Buddy Bolden" (New Orleans: Hogan Jazz Archive, Tulane University). The City Directory of 1903 gives the address of the Ladies' Providence Benevolent Association Hall as 2241 South Liberty, in uptown New Orleans.

36. Fred Ramsey, "Correspondence, Oxford University Press, June 14, 1974, Box 17B," in MSS 559 (New Orleans: Williams Research Center, Historic New Orleans Collection).

37. Fred Ramsey, "Correspondence, Oxford University Press, March 17, 1976, Box 17B," in MSS 559 (New Orleans: Williams Research Center, Historic New Orleans Collection).

38. Fred Ramsey, "Correspondence, Oxford University Press, Dec 29 & 30, 1977, Box 17 B," in MSS 559 (New Orleans: Williams Research Center, Historic New Orleans Collection).

39. Sheldon Meyer, "Correspondence, Oxford University Press, January 8, 1979, Box 17 B," in MSS 559 (New Orleans: Williams Research Center, Historic New Orleans Collection).

40. William Ivy Hair, *Carnival of Fury: Robert Charles and the New Orleans Race Riot of 1900* (Baton Rouge: Louisiana State University Press, 1976), 119–20.

41. *Ibid.*, 1.

42. Fred Ramsey, "Foreword to *Buddy Bolden and His New Orleans* (unpublished), dated April 25, 1977, Box 10 A," in MSS 559 (New Orleans: Williams Research Center, Historic New Orleans Collection).

43. Marshall W. Stearns, *The Story of Jazz* (London: Sedgwick and Jackson, 1957), 55–56.

44. Alan Lomax, *Mister Jelly Roll: The Fortunes of Jelly Roll Morton, New Orleans Creole and "Inventor of Jazz"* (New York: Duell, Sloan and Pearce, 1950), 69; Adam Gussow, *Seems Like Murder Here: Southern Violence and the Blues Tradition* (Chicago: University of Chicago Press, 2002), 176.

45. Frederic Ramsey Jr., "Fred Ramsey Speaks Out," *78 Quarterly* VI, no. 4 (1988): 37.

46. Marquis, *In Search of Buddy Bolden*, 153.

47. Hobson, *American Jazz Music*, 58.

48. Mr. and Mrs. Vernon Castle, *Modern Dancing* (New York: Harper & Row, 1914; reprint, New York: Da Capo, 1980).

49. Carl Engel, "Jazz: A Musical Discussion," *Atlantic Monthly*, August 1922; Karl Koenig, *Evolution of Ragtime and Blues to Jazz* (Running Springs, CA: Basin Street Books, undated), 101.

50. Ramsey and Smith, *Jazzmen*, 13.

51. Rudi Blesh and Harriet Janis, *They All Played Ragtime: The True Story of an American Music* (London: Sedgwick and Jackson, 1950; reprint, 1960), 77–78.

52. Jelly Roll Morton, "Transcript of the 1938 Library of Congress Recordings of Jelly Roll Morton," ed. John Szwed (Washington: Library of Congress, 2006), 51.

53. *Ibid.*, 52.

54. Barney and Seymore, "The St. Louis Tickle" (1904), Performing Arts Reading Room, Library of Congress.

55. David A. Jasen and Trebor Jay Tichenor, *Rags and Ragtime: A Musical History* (New York: Seabury Press, 1978), 46–47; Peter C. Muir, "Before 'Crazy Blues': Commercial Blues in America 1850–1920" (diss., City University of New York, 2004), 352.

56. Marquis, *In Search of Buddy Bolden*, 109.

57. *Ibid.*, 111.

58. Edmond Souchon, "King Oliver: A Very Personal Memory," *Jazz Review* 3, no. 4 (1960).

59. Goffin, *La Nouvelle-Orléans Capital Du Jazz*, 83.

60. Blesh and Janis, *They All Played Ragtime*, 77–78.

61. Beatrice Alcorn interview, June 23, 1971, in Marquis, *In Search of Buddy Bolden: First Man of Jazz*, 94. There are reports of Lorenzo Staultz (guitarist) improvising vocals with Bolden's band probably around 1906. *Ibid.*, 78–79.

62. Jelly Roll Morton, "Buddy Bolden's Blues," recorded December 16, 1939, New York (General 403A, Commodore 589A).

63. Joseph E. Fogarty, "Interview Transcript June 18, 1969," ed. William Russell and William Hogan (New Orleans: William Ransom Hogan Jazz Archive, Tulane University).

64. *Ibid.*

65. Frankie Duson's name is sometimes spelled Dusen.

66. Marquis, *In Search of Buddy Bolden*, 110.

67. Danny Barker and Alyn Shipton, *Buddy Bolden and the Last Days of Storyville* (London and New York: Cassell, 1998), ix.

68. Dude Bottley, "Interview, 1955," *ibid.*, 9.

69. Lawrence Gushee, "Would You Believe Ferman Mouton?" *Storyville* 98 (1981): 56–59.

70. Marquis, *In Search of Buddy Bolden*, 110.

71. E. Belfield Spriggins, "Excavating Local Jazz," *Louisiana Weekly*, April 22, 1933. Abbott, "Remembering Mr. E. Belfield Spriggins," 14.

72. Susie Farr, "Interview Notes, July 25, 1967," ed. Richard Allen (New Orleans: William Ransom Hogan Jazz Archive, Tulane University).

73. Marquis, *In Search of Buddy Bolden*, 65.

74. Marquis's footnote: Edouard Henriques, notary public, February 6, 1907, minutes of a meeting of the Union Sons Benevolent Association that includes a list of officers elected on November 9, 1904, in Notarial [*sic*] Archives, Civil District Courts Building, New Orleans, *ibid.*, 68.

75. Eddie Dawson, "Interview Digest June 28, 1961," ed. William Russell and Ralph Collins (New Orleans: William Ransom Hogan Jazz Archive, Tulane University); Eddie Garland, "Interview Digest August 8, 1958," ed. William Russell (New Orleans: William Ransom Hogan Jazz Archive, Tulane University); Joseph "Wooden Joe" Nicholas, "Interview Digest, November 12, 1956," ed. William Russell and Charlie DeVore (New Orleans: William Ransom Hogan Jazz Archive, Tulane University).

76. Manuel Manetta, "Interview Digest, March 28, 1957," ed. William Russell, et al. (New Orleans: William Ransom Hogan Jazz Archive, Tulane University).

77. Ramsey and Smith, *Jazzmen*, 15.

78. Barker and Shipton, *Buddy Bolden and the Last Days of Storyville*, 22.

79. *Ibid.*, 23.

80. Ramsey and Smith, *Jazzmen*, 13.

81. William J. Schafer and Johannes Riedel, *The Art of Ragtime: Form and Meaning of an Original Black American Art* (Baton Rouge: Louisiana State University Press, 1973; reprint, 1974), 149.

82. Blesh and Janis, *They All Played Ragtime*, 77.

83. Marquis, *In Search of Buddy Bolden*, 79–80.

84. Karl Koenig, *Trinity of Early Jazz Leaders: John Robichaux, 'Toots' Johnson, Claiborne Williams* (Running Springs, CA: Basin Street Books, undated), 19.

85. *Ibid.*, 19.

86. *Ibid.*, 21.

87. *New York Clipper*, November 4, 1905 (Lynn Abbott's notes).

88. *Indianapolis Freeman*, October 21, 1905 (Lynn Abbott's notes).

89. The similarity of Scott Joplin's "Sarah Dear," Ben Harney's "Cake-Walk in the Sky," and Theron C. Bennet's "The St. Louis Tickle" is noted in Edward A. Berlin, *King of Ragtime: Scott Joplin and His Era* (New York and Oxford: Oxford University Press, 1994).

90. William H. Tallmadge, "Ben Harney: The Middlesborough Years, 1890-93," *American Music* 13, no. 2 (1995): 173.

91. Lynn Abbott, "'A Worthy Copy of the Subject He Mimics.' Ben Harney in Context, 1896-1898," *Rag-Time Ephemeralist* 3 (2002): 42.

92. Schenkerian theorists would argue that all tonal music, however long or complex, is a prolongation of a perfect cadence. Heinrich Schenker, *Free Composition (Der Freie Satz)*, trans. Ernst Oster (New York: Longman, 1979).

93. "Jazz: A Musical Discussion," *Atlantic Monthly*, August 1922; Koenig, *Evolution of Ragtime and Blues to Jazz*, 101.

CHAPTER 3

1. Mike Hazeldine and Barry Martyn, *Bunk Johnson: Song of the Wanderer* (New Orleans: Jazzology Press, 2000), 50.

2. *Ibid.*, 51.

3. "This Isn't Bunk; Bunk Taught Louis," *Down Beat*, June 1939, 4.

4. Ramsey and Smith, *Jazzmen*.

5. *Ibid.*, 24.

6. *Ibid.*, 24–25.

7. Marquis, *In Search of Buddy Bolden*.

8. Unidentified author, "'Jazz Flashbacks,' *Basin Street NJF* (New Orleans) Vol. 2 no. 2, February 1946, Box 20A," in MSS 559 (New Orleans: Williams Research Center, Historic New Orleans Collection).

9. It is probable that the term "blues" is being applied retrospectively by Bunk Johnson. The term was used in popular song from the mid-1800s to describe a melancholy disposition, but use of the term "blues" to describe a type of music first appeared as a subtitle to Robert Hoffman's "I'm Alabama Bound" (1909). This was subtitled "The Alabama Blues." Lynn Abbott and Doug Seroff, "'They Cert'ly Sound Good to Me': Sheet Music, Southern Vaudeville, and the Commercial Ascendancy of the Blues," *American Music* 14, no. 4 (1996). Albert Glenny (b. 1870) remembered "I'm Alabama Bound" to be a "real blues" that he recalled from around 1904; Albert Glenny, "Interview Transcript, March 27, 1957," ed. Richard B. Allen and Nesuhi Ertegun (New Orleans: William Ransom Hogan Jazz Archive, Tulane University).

10. "Johnson Baseball Park and Lincoln Park," Box 22 B in MSS 559 (New Orleans: Williams Research Center, Historic New Orleans Collection).

11. Johnson, George W. saloon 7933 Oleander, Soards' New Orleans City Directory, 1904 (New Orleans: Williams Research Center, Historic New Orleans Collection).

12. Ferrand and Mathilda Clementine, "Interview Digest, November 29, 1974, Box 5 B," in MSS 559 (New Orleans: Williams Research Center, Historic New Orleans Collection).

13. This is consistent with fire insurance maps for 1908 that show the building.

14. Clementine, "Interview Digest, November 29, 1974, Box 5 B."

15. *Ibid.*

16. Cornish, "*Jazzmen* Interviews, Box 16 C."

17. Hazeldine and Martyn, *Bunk Johnson*, 22.

18. Fred Ramsey, "Letter to Bill Russell, August 2, 1977," in MSS 519 (New Orleans: Williams Research Center, Historic New Orleans Collection).

19. Mike Hazeldine, "Bunk Johnson: The Story So Far," *New Orleans Music* 14, no. 1 (2008): 12.

20. Notable among these: Mike Hazeldine, Barry Martyn, and Lawrence Gushee.

21. Hazeldine, "Bunk Johnson: The Story So Far," 17. I am not convinced that the 1930 census quoted is correct. There is a Willie G. Johnson (aged 40), husband of Martha Johnson and father to Alonzo Nathanial Johnson, in the Baton Rouge 1930 Census, Ward 1, District 17-3, Supervisor's District 6, Sheet 19A.

22. Lawrence Gushee, "When Was Bunk Johnson Born and Why Should We Care?" *The Jazz Archivist: A Newsletter of the William Ransom Hogan Jazz Archive* II, no. 2 (1987).

23. Hazeldine and Martyn, *Bunk Johnson*, 21.

24. *Ibid.*, 11.

25. Theresa Johnson and Millie Young were living together at 2719 St. Thomas Street in 1899 Soards' New Orleans City Directory.

26. I have subsequently learned from www.doctorjazz.co.uk/portnewor.html that Geary Johnson died of pulmonary consumption on September 30, 1892 (Orleans Parish Death Records, volume 102, page 897).

27. *Seventy Years of Service: New Orleans University* (New Orleans University, 1935), 11 (Dillard University Archives).

28. *Seventy Years of Service: New Orleans University* (New Orleans University, 1935), 13 (Dillard University Archives).

29. Bunk Johnson, "Transcript of Bunk's Talking Session—June 13, 1942, Folder 141," in MSS 512 (New Orleans: Williams Research Center, Historic New Orleans Collection).

30. *Yearbook of the University of New Orleans 1880–81* (Dillard University Archives).

31. Gushee, "When Was Bunk Johnson Born and Why Should We Care?" 6.

32. *Ibid.*, 6. The only William Johnson that I have found first appeared in the 1883–84 and the 1888–89 yearbooks. William A. Johnson was a student of the Grammar Department. His address is given as "131 Constantinople N.O." This is not an address associated with Bunk, who lived further uptown and closer to the river.

33. Bunk Johnson, "Interview Notes, October 23, 1945, folder 215," in MSS 512 (New Orleans: Williams Research Center, Historic New Orleans Collection).

34. Sanborn fire insurance map of New Orleans, 1896.

35. Soards' City Directory, New Orleans, 1893.

36. *Ibid.*, 1890.

37. In Soards' City Directory 1897 and 1898 the address is given as the corner of Laurel and Belleville. This should read Bellecastle. In 1899 the address is given as 5243 Laurel.

38. By 1900 Ezekiel Warmington was living with his wife of twelve years, Celestine, and five sons at 620 Bellecastle. This was around the corner from the church. He was 43 years old (b. April 1857), and gave his occupation as "Minister"; Twelfth Census of the United States: 1900, New Orleans, Ward 13, District 125, sheet 18. By 1910 he was ministering in a "Baptist Church" in Pass Christian (Ward 3), Harrison County, Mississippi; Thirteenth Census of the United States: 1910, Pass Christian City, Ward 3, sheet 16A (Ancestry.com).

39. The French "Sacristain" translates to sexton or church caretaker. Goffin, *La Nouvelle-Orléans Capital Du Jazz*, 97. David Evans informs me that "Coochie" is a common African American nickname, as in Muddy Waters's "Hoochie Coochie Man" (Chess 1560). David Evans, *Big Road Blues: Tradition and Creativity in the Folk Blues* (Da Capo Press, 1982; reprint, 1987), 135. "It refers to a woman's pelvic or genital region and would represent the 'interest' of the man having this nickname." If this is a nickname, it would go some way to explain why searches of city directories and other records have not produced anything conclusive.

40. Bunk Johnson, "Letter to Bill Russell giving further information for *Jazzmen* (1939), folder 135," in MSS 512 (New Orleans: Williams Research Center, Historic New Orleans Collection).

41. By this time the Reverend Warmington had moved to 5004 Freret Street.

42. Goffin, *La Nouvelle-Orléans Capital Du Jazz*, 96–99.

43. Nat Shapiro and Nat Hentoff, *Hear Me Talkin' to Ya: The Story of Jazz by the Men Who Made It* (London: Penguin, 1955; reprint, 1962), 66.

44. Lomax, *Mister Jelly Roll*, 35.

45. Lawrence Gushee, "A Preliminary Chronology of the Early Career of Ferd 'Jelly Roll' Morton," *American Music* 3, no. 4 (1985): 392.

46. AFC 1938/001 (F1) subfolder 1 (American Folklife Center, Library of Congress).

47. *Ibid.*

48. Joseph French Johnson, "The Crisis and Panic of 1907," *Political Science Quarterly* 23, no. 3 (1908): 454–67.

49. Shapiro and Hentoff, *Hear Me Talkin' to Ya*, 66.

50. Anthony Clark, "State of Louisiana versus Timothy Mercedes, Box 22B, Masonic Hall," in MSS 559 (New Orleans: Williams Research Center, Historic New Orleans Collection).

51. Jelly Roll Morton recalled pianists Albert Carroll and Tony Jackson in the Library of Congress recordings. He also said he learned to play piano from a Frank Richards, and credited him with co-authoring "New Orleans Blues." Lomax, *Mister Jelly Roll*, 62.

52. Bunk Johnson, "Interview notes with Gus [?] October 23, 1945, Folder 215," in MSS 512 (New Orleans: Williams Research Center, Historic New Orleans Collection). It could be that his grandmother had more than one address on this block, or perhaps let rooms, because in the 1900 census Peter Sampson, a day laborer, along with his wife Clara and two daughters Florence and Geneva, lived at this address; Twelfth Census of the United States, 1900, Parish of Orleans, Louisiana, Ward 13, First Precinct, Sheet 23 B. Soards' City Directories of New Orleans 1886, 1891, 1892, and 1893 give a Peter Sampson "lab[orer]" residing at Coliseum Street between Cadiz and Valence. In 1897, 1898, and 1899 Peter Sampson "lab" is at 817 Jena.

53. Bunk Johnson, "Letter to David Stuart, August 28, 1941," in MSS 506 (New Orleans: Williams Research Center, Historic New Orleans Collection).

54. Henry T. Sampson, *Blacks in Blackface: A Source Book on Early Black Musical Shows* (Metuchen, NJ, and London: Scarecrow Press, 1980), 103.

55. Rose and Souchon, *New Orleans Jazz*, 95.

56. Joe Oliver, "Letter to William 'Bunk' Johnson, February 15, 1930, Box 9B," in MSS 559 (New Orleans: Williams Research Center, Historic New Orleans Collection).

57. Volume 33, page 460, New Orleans, Louisiana, Marriage Records Index, 1831-1925 (Ancestry.com). Stella told her interviewers that she was married in 1912.

58. Stella Oliver, "Interview Digest, April 22, 1959," ed. William Russell and Ralph Collins (New Orleans: William Ransom Hogan Jazz Archive, Tulane University).

59. Souchon, "King Oliver: A Very Personal Memory," 8.

60. *Ibid.*, 9.

61. According to Oliver's wife, Stella, his mother died; she is less clear about his father.

62. Oliver, "Interview Digest, April 22, 1959."

63. *Ibid.*

64. Clarence "Little Dad" Vincent, "Interview Digest, November 17, 1959," ed. Richard B. Allen (New Orleans: William Ransom Hogan Jazz Archive, Tulane University).

65. Bertha McCullem, "Audio Interview," ed. William Russell, Harold Dejan, and Ralph Collins (New Orleans: William Ransom Hogan Jazz Archive, Tulane University).

66. In the 1900 census, George's year of birth is 1883; it is estimated at 1884 in the 1910 census, 1885 in the 1920 census, and July 28, 1883, on his World War I draft card (Ancestry.com).

67. Bunk Johnson, "Folder 141," in MSS 512 (New Orleans: Historic New Orleans Collection, Williams Research Center).

68. Rose and Souchon, *New Orleans Jazz*, 20.

69. Bunk Johnson, "Folder 141," in MSS 512 (New Orleans: Williams Research Center, Historic New Orleans Collection).

70. Oliver, "Interview Digest, April 22, 1959."

71. Eddie Dawson, "Interview Digest August 11, 1959," ed. William Russell and Ralph Collins (New Orleans: William Ransom Hogan Jazz Archive, Tulane University).

72. Jelly Roll Morton, "Letter to Roy Carew, June 22, 1938 [1939], Folder 55," in MSS 507 (New Orleans: Williams Research Center, Historic New Orleans Collection).

73. Jelly Roll Morton, "I Created Jazz in 1902, Not W. C. Handy," *Down Beat*, August 1938.

74. Sidney Bechet and Manuel Perez et al., "Interview Digest, June 1944 and November 19, 1945," ed. John Reid and Richard B. Allen (New Orleans: William Ransom Hogan Jazz Archive, Tulane University).

75. Cornish, "*Jazzmen* Interviews, Box 16 C."

76. Lynn Abbott interviews with Rev. Morris Burrell, July 11, 1981, and December 28, 1984; Rev. Mitchell Oleavia, July 26 and September 8, 1981; Rose and Souchon, *New Orleans Jazz*, 95; Sam Charters, *Jazz New Orleans, 1885–1963*, 7; Austin M. Sonnier Jr., *Willie 'Bunk' Johnson*, 3; *Religious Recordings from Black New Orleans 1924–1931*, ed. Lynn Abbott, 504, Record Productions, LP 20, 1989 (sleeve notes).

77. Soards' New Orleans Directory, 1900 through 1912; Lynn Abbott interviews with Rev. Morris Burrell, July 11, 1981, and December 28, 1984; *Religious Recordings from Black New Orleans 1924-1931*, ed. Abbott (sleeve notes).

78. Hazeldine and Martyn, *Bunk Johnson*, 108.

79. *Ibid.*, 21–22.

80. Cornish, "*Jazzmen* Interviews, Box 16 C."

CHAPTER 4

1. Gerhard Kubik, "The African Matrix in Jazz Harmonic Practice," *Black Music Research Journal* 25, no. 1 (2005): 168.

2. Frederika Bremer, *The Homes of the New World: Impressions of America* (New York: Harper Bros., 1853); Gage Averill, *Four Parts, No Waiting: A Social History of Barbershop Harmony* (New York: Oxford University Press, 2003), 30.

3. James Earl Henry, "The Origins of Barbershop Harmony: A Study of Barbershop's Musical Link to Other African American Musics as Evidenced through Recordings and Arrangements of Early Black and White Quartets" (diss., Washington University, 2000), 203–4.

4. William Francis Allen, Charles Pickard Ware, and Lucy McKim Garrison, *Slave Songs of the United States* (New York: Dover, 1867; reprint, 1995), v; see also Lynn Abbott and Doug Seroff, *Out of Sight: The Rise of African American Popular Music 1889–1895* (Jackson: University Press of Mississippi, 2002), 358–60.

5. Allen, Ware, and Garrison, *Slave Songs of the United States*, iv–v.

6. *Ibid.*, xxi.

7. Abbott, "'Play That Barber Shop Chord,'" 290.

8. Billy McClain, "The Man Who Originated the Cake Walk," *Indianapolis Freeman*, April 23, 1910; *ibid.*, 290.

9. James Weldon Johnson and J. Rosamond Johnson, *The Books of American Negro Spirituals* (New York: Da Capo, 1925, 1926; reprint, 1969), 35.

10. Lewis F. Muir and William Tracey, "Play that Barbershop Chord" (1910) (Performing Arts Reading Room, Library of Congress).

11. Lynn Abbott interview with Dr. Laddie Melton, Beaumont, Texas, May 27, 1983; Abbott, "'Play That Barber Shop Chord,'" 290.

12. Spaeth, *Barber Shop Ballads: A Book of Close Harmony*, 17.

13. Spaeth, *Barber Shop Ballads and How to Sing Them*, 6.

14. Allen, Ware, and Garrison, *Slave Songs of the United States*, v–vi.

15. Both the first tenor and lead actually sound an octave below where written. It is the convention in close harmony barbershop to write the lead and tenor parts an octave above the sounding pitch for the sake of clarity. I have indicated this in the clef.

16. R. Emmet Kennedy, *Mellows: A Chronicle of Unknown Singers* (New York: A. and C. Boni, 1925), 30.

17. Roy Carew, Letter to the *Washington Post*, May 6, 1938. The response was recorded in the foreword to William Russell's *"Oh Mister Jelly!": A Jelly Roll Morton Scrapbook* (Copenhagen: Jazz Media, 1999), a book that Russell claimed "Roy Carew should have written."

18. Roy Carew in William Russell, *"Oh, Mister Jelly!"* 14–15; unpublished manuscript, "Carew, Roy, Folder 176," in MSS 519 (New Orleans: Williams Research Center, Historic New Orleans Collection).

19. R. Emmet Kennedy, *The Songs of Aengus* (New Orleans: Myers' Printing House, 1910).

20. R. Emmet Kennedy, Foreword, *Remnants of Noah's Ham* (According to Genesis) (New Orleans: Myers' Printing House, 1910).

21. Kennedy, *Mellows*, 179.

22. Program of *Dress Rehearsal*, May 18, 1909, Karl Koenig, *The Scrap Book of R. Emmet Kennedy* (Running Springs, CA: Basin Street Books, 2007).

23. Gus Cannon, "Poor Boy Long Way from Home," recorded Chicago, November 1927, Paramount 12571.

24. This is a transposed version for ease of comparison.

25. Spaeth, *Barber Shop Ballads and How to Sing Them*, 12.

26. Steve Brown, "Interview Transcript, April 22, 1958," ed. Richard Allen and William Russell (New Orleans: William Ransom Hogan Jazz Archive, Tulane University).

27. "Transcript of the 1938 Library of Congress Recordings of Jelly Roll Morton," ed. John Szwed (2006), 28.

28. *Ibid.*, 29.

29. Louis Armstrong, *Satchmo: My Life in New Orleans* (Peter Davies, 1955; reprint, Sedgwick and Jackson, 1957), 81.

30. Baby Dodds and Larry Gara, *The Baby Dodds Story*, rev. ed. (Baton Rouge: Louisiana State University Press, 1992), 2.

31. Lee Collins, *Oh, Didn't He Ramble: The Life Story of Lee Collins*, ed. Mary Collins (Urbana: University of Illinois Press, 1974), 62; Abbott, "'Play That Barber Shop Chord,'" 314.

32. Lemon Nash, "Interview Digest, September 28, 1960," ed. Richard B. Allen and Marjorie T. Zander (New Orleans: William Ransom Hogan Jazz Archive, Tulane University).

33. Jones and Wise, "Interview Transcript, June 4, 1954, Box 9 B."

34. *Ibid.*

CHAPTER 5

1. Bill Russell, *New Orleans Style* (New Orleans: Jazzology Press, 1994), 8–9.

2. Bill Russell, "Bunk Johnson," *Jazz Quarterly* (Fall 1942), in Hazeldine and Martyn, *Bunk Johnson*, 265.

3. William Wagner, "Bunk and My Brother," *ibid.*, 269.

4. I have been unable to locate the Cornish interview in Russell's papers at the Historic New Orleans Collection. Hazeldine and Martyn had knowledge of Russell's copy of this interview; see *Bunk Johnson*, 12. The only copy that I know of is in Frederic Ramsey's papers also held at Historic New Orleans Collection. The Ramsey papers did not become available to researchers until the Historic New Orleans Collection acquired them in 2006.

5. In principle, all of the contributors to *Jazzmen* would have known this; Stephen Smith's wife, Lee, circulated the notes among all the contributors. Raeburn, *New Orleans Style and the Writing of American Jazz History*, 61.

6. See Mike Hazeldine and Bill Russell, *Bill Russell's American Music* (New Orleans: Jazzology Press, 1993); Hazeldine and Martyn, *Bunk Johnson*.

7. Peter Bocage, "Interview Digest, February 5, 1962," ed. Barry Martyn and Richard Knowles (New Orleans: William Ransom Hogan Jazz Archive, Tulane University).

8. Hazeldine and Martyn, *Bunk Johnson*, 48–49.

9. Bunk often used a mute when practicing.

10. Lee Collins, quoted in Hazeldine and Martyn, *Bunk Johnson*, 50. Lee Collins replaced Armstrong in Joe "King" Oliver's band when Armstrong left to join Fletcher Henderson in New York.

11. The chords and melody are as given in David W. Littlefield, ed., *Dixieland Fake Book* Vol. 1 (2000).

12. Gunther Schuller, *Early Jazz: Its Roots and Musical Development* (Oxford: Oxford University Press, 1986), 83.

13. Spaeth, *Barber Shop Ballads: A Book of Close Harmony*, 19.

14. Armstrong, *Swing*, 4; Meryman, *Louis Armstrong*, 13; Armstrong, *Satchmo*, 30; Abbott, "'Play That Barber Shop Chord,'" 315.

15. Armstrong, *Satchmo*; Abbott, "'Play That Barber Shop Chord,'" 318.

16. Armstrong, *Satchmo*, 86.

17. Hazeldine and Russell, *Bill Russell's American Music*, 1.

18. I have added the implied harmony.

19. Bunk Johnson, "Buddy Bolden's Style," AM LP 643 (recorded June 13, 1942, New Orleans).

20. Howard Odum, "Folk-Song and Folk-Poetry as Found in the Secular Songs of the Southern Negroes," *Journal of American Folklore* 24, no. 93 (1911): 256.

21. E. C. Perrow, "Songs and Rhymes from the South," *Journal of American Folklore* 28, no. 108 (1915): 147.

22. *Ibid.*, 147.

23. Nicholas, "Interview Digest, November 12, 1956."

24. Dorothy Scarborough, "The 'Blues' as Folk Song," Folklore Society of Texas, 1916; Koenig, *Evolution of Ragtime and Blues to Jazz*, 117–18.

25. "New Sounds from the Crib House," in *Esquire's World of Jazz* (London: Arthur Baker, 1962).

26. John Joseph, "Interview Transcript, November 24, 1958," ed. William Russell, Richard B. Allen, and Nesuhi Ertegun (New Orleans: William Ransom Hogan Jazz Archive, Tulane University).

27. *Ibid.*

28. *Ibid.*

29. My italics; Abbe Niles, "Notes to the collection," 1947 edition, W. C. Handy, *Blues: An Anthology* (New York: Macmillan, 1926; reprint, 1974), 206.

30. My italics; *ibid.*, 17.

31. Nicholas, "Interview Digest, November 12, 1956."

32. When Nicholas recorded the tune in Artesian Hall on May 10, 1945, he did so for Bill Russell's American Music label. Most members of the ensemble that Bill Russell brought together for this recording were older New Orleans musicians: Wooden Joe Nicholas (tpt, b. 1883); Jim Robinson (tbn, b. 1892); Albert Burbank (clt, b. 1902); Lawrence Marrero (bjo, b. 1900); Austin Young (sbs, b. 1885) (source for dates: Rose and Souchon, *New Orleans Jazz*).

33. Author's transcription of Wooden Joe Nicholas, "Careless Love," recorded Artesian Hall, New Orleans, May 10, 1945 (American Music MX803).

34. Stephen Calt, *I'd Rather Be the Devil: Skip James and the Blues* (New York: Da Capo, 1994), 35–36.

35. *Ibid.*, 39.

36. Evans, *Big Road Blues*, 44.

37. In European tonal harmony there is a family of augmented sixth chords (German sixth, French sixth, Italian sixth) that have harmonic features similar to those of the barbershop sixth.

38. Willem Weijts, "Bunk Johnson: Discography" http://www.weijts.scarlet.nl/bjd.htm, 2010.

39. Dodds and Gara, *The Baby Dodds Story*, 34–35.

40. Bill Russell, "Interview, Feb 2, 1975"; "Interview, October 1993" (New Orleans: William Ransom Hogan Jazz Archive, Tulane University).

41. John McCusker, "Ory Baptismal Certificate," *Jazz Archivist: A Newsletter of the William Ransom Hogan Jazz Archive* IX, no. 2 (1994); John McCusker, "Le Monde Creole: The Early Life of Kid Ory," *Jazz Archivist: A Newsletter of the William Ransom Hogan Jazz Archive* XX (2007); Edward "Kid" Ory, "Interview Transcript, April 20, 1957 (for *Life Magazine*)," ed. Nesuhi Ertegun and Robert Campbell (New Orleans: William Ransom Hogan Jazz Archive, Tulane University).

42. Ory, "Interview Transcript, April 20, 1957 (for *Life Magazine*)."

43. *Ibid.*

44. Lawrence Duhé, "Interview Digest, 1960," ed. George Brown (New Orleans: William Ransom Hogan Jazz Archive, Tulane University); Morris French, "Interview Digest, June 24, 1960," ed. Richard B. Allen and Marjorie T. Zander (New Orleans: William Ransom Hogan Jazz Archive, Tulane University).

45. Ory, "Interview Transcript, April 20, 1957 (for *Life Magazine*)."

46. Jane Bowers and William Westcott, "Mama Yancey and the Revival Blues Tradition," *Black Music Research Journal* 12, no. 2 (1992): 175.

47. *Ibid.*, 175; Trebor Jay Tichenor, *Ragtime Rarities* (New York: Dover, 1975), 33–37.

48. W. C. Handy, *Father of the Blues* (London: Sedgwick & Jackson, 1941; reprint, 1961), 78. Handy would later publish "Make Me a Pallet on Your Floor" titled "Atlanta Blues" (1924). Handy, *Blues: An Anthology*, 139–41.

49. Howard Odum, "Folk-Song and Folk-Poetry as Found in the Secular Songs of the Southern Negroes (Concluded)," *Journal of American Folklore* 24, no. 94 (1911): 396.

50. Jelly Roll Morton, "Transcript of the 1938 Library of Congress Recordings of Jelly Roll Morton," ed. John Szwed (Washington: Library of Congress, 2006), 79.

51. "Bolden Medley," *Bunk Johnson in San Francisco*, AMCD-16.

52. For more on Ory's early years see John McCusker, *Creole Trombone: Kid Ory and the Early Years of Jazz* (Jackson: University Press of Mississippi, 2012).

53. Ory, "Interview Transcript, April 20, 1957 (for *Life Magazine*)." This is probably Henry Peyton (sometimes called Billy Peyton). Ferrand Clementin, "Interview Digest August 2, 1973," ed. Richard B. Allen (New Orleans: William Ransom Hogan Jazz Archive, Tulane University). Ory does say in the interview that he was not sure of Peyton's first name. There was also Dave Peyton, a piano player and arranger that worked with Ory in Chicago. This may (in part) explain Ory's confusion.

54. Ory, "Interview Transcript, April 20, 1957 (for *Life Magazine*)."

55. Marquis, *In Search of Buddy Bolden*, 40. Marquis identifies two brothers, William and Henry Peyton, both of whom were musicians, in Donald M. Marquis, "The Bolden-Peyton Legend—a Re-Valuation," *Jazz Journal* 30 (1977): 24.

56. John Joseph, "Interview Transcript November 26, 1958" (New Orleans: William Ransom Hogan Jazz Archive, Tulane University).

57. Jones, "Interview Transcript, Jan 19, 1959." Hugh "Hughie" Rankin may have been Peyton's guitarist. Eddie Dawson, "Interview Digest April 5, 1972," ed. Richard B. Allen (New Orleans: William Ransom Hogan Jazz Archive, Tulane University).

58. Jones, "Interview Transcript, Jan 19, 1959."

59. Joseph, "Interview Transcript, November 26, 1958."

60. Willie "Old Man" Parker, "Interview Transcript, November 7, 1958," ed. Richard B. Allen (New Orleans: William Ransom Hogan Jazz Archive, Tulane University).

61. Dawson, "Interview Digest June 28, 1961."

62. Dawson, "Interview Digest August 11, 1959."

63. Dawson, "Interview Digest June 28, 1961."

64. Dawson, "Interview Digest August 11, 1959."

65. *Ibid.* He also says that "Rabbit" Brown and Walter Preston (b. 1888, according to WWI draft card at Ancestry.com) were among two of the earliest blues guitar players in New Orleans.

66. Ramsey and Smith, *Jazzmen*, 13.

67. Cornish, "*Jazzmen* Interviews, Box 16 C."

68. Jelly Roll Morton, "Mamie's Blues," recorded New York, December 16, 1939 (General 4001, Commodore Music Shop 587, Vogue V-2122), Jazz Section 695, Brian Rust, *Jazz Records 1897–1942* (Chigwell, UK: Storyville, 1969; reprint, 1975), 1168.

69. Lomax, *Mister Jelly Roll!*, 20–21. On March 25, 1879, Clementine Walker gave birth to Mary Celina Desdunes; the birth record gives the father as "Rudolphe L." New Orleans, Louisiana, Birth Records Index, 1790–1899, Vol. 74, 79 (Ancestry.com). Rudolphe L. Desdunes appears in the 1880 Census, described as "mulatto," married with a young family and working as a clerk. 1880 United States Census, Parish of Orleans, New Orleans, page 53, lines 29–35 (Ancestry.com). Clementine was his mistress and Clementine's children took their father's name. Rudolphe Lucien Desdunes would later become a prominent campaigner and writer in support of Creoles of Color. Rudolphe Lucien Desdunes, *Our People and Our History: Fifty Creole Portraits*, trans. Sister Dorothea Olga McCants (Baton Rouge: Louisiana State University Press, 1911; reprint, 1973).

70. As it appears on his baptismal certificate. Gushee, "A Preliminary Chronology of the Early Career of Ferd 'Jelly Roll' Morton."

71. Jelly Roll Morton, "From a typewritten reproduction of an article in Jelly Roll's hand in the Tempo Music files, prompted by an April 1938 article in *Down Beat* by Marshall Stearns," "Folder 134," in MSS 506 (New Orleans: Williams Research Center, Historic New Orleans Collection).

72. She was living under her married name Mary Degay. Hobson, "New Orleans Jazz and the Blues," 8; Peter Hanley, www.doctorjazz.co.uk/portnewor.html.

73. 2706 South Robertson Street (the 1900 census); 2621 Fourth Street (Soards' City Directory).

74. Gushee, "A Preliminary Chronology of the Early Career of Ferd 'Jelly Roll' Morton," 394.

75. Unfortunately, further searches have proved inconclusive. By 1905 Laura Hunter was recorded in the City Directory as living at 1619 Magnolia. Moreover, I have not found another address for Mamie Desdunes until the 1910 census, when she was living at 2414 Clara Street.

76. R2573 "Mamie's Blues," New York, December 16, 1939, General 4001, Commodore Music Shop 587, Vogue V-2122, Jazz Section 695, Brian Rust, *Jazz Records 1897–1942* (Chigwell, UK: Storyville, 1969; reprint, 1975), 1168.

77. Charles Edward Smith, "Quoting Jelly Roll Morton, Folder 202," in MSS 506 (New Orleans: Williams Research Center, Historic New Orleans Collection); Russell, *"Oh, Mister Jelly."*

78. Richard M. Jones: 101681-1 "Trouble in Mind," Chicago, August 5, 1936, Bluebird B-6569, Rust, *Jazz Records 1897–1942*, 911; Bertha "Chippie" Hill: 9510-B "Trouble in Mind," Chicago, February 23, 1926, Okeh 8312, *ibid.*, 793.

79. Roger Wood, *Texas Zydeco* (Austin: University of Texas Press, 2006), 67.

80. Bunk Johnson, "Interview with Alan Lomax March 1949, Box 33B," in MSS 559 (New Orleans: Williams Research Center, Historic New Orleans Collection). As far as is known, this interview was recorded on a tape that does not survive. Nor does the Historic New Orleans Collection have a complete transcript. This excerpt is punctuated differently from the version that appears in *Mister Jelly Roll*. It is likely that at some time Ramsey may have had access to the original tape or an alternative transcript. Bill Russell may also have had access to the full interview.

81. Perry Bradford, *Born with the Blues* (New York: Oak Publications, 1965), 32.

82. Roy Carew, "Typescript 'Jelly Roll Morton and his Library of Congress Recordings' circa 1949–Feb 1950," "Carew, Roy, Folder 158," in MSS 519 (New Orleans: Williams Research Center, Historic New Orleans Collection).

83. Lomax, *Mister Jelly Roll*, 248.

84. Bradford, *Born with the Blues*, 34. I am indebted to David Evans for directing me toward the 1928 recordings of Virginia songster and barber William "Bill" Moore. His recording of "One Way Gal" (Paramount 12648) has both the *"She walked in the rain, 'till her feet got soakin' wet"* and also *"If you can't give a dollar give me a lousy dime"* verse, but without to the 2:19 lyric, in sixteen-bar form. There is some controversy as to whether this is the same Bill Moore that recorded "Old Country Rock" (Paramount 12761). The guitar picking style is quite similar (although arguably less complex) and the spoken interjects are quite different.

85. Lynn Abbott and Doug Seroff, *Ragged but Right: Black Travelling Shows, "Coon Songs," and the Dark Pathway to Blues and Jazz* (Jackson: University Press of Mississippi, 2007), 409–10 f99.

86. *Ibid.*, 229.

87. March 4, 1922, *Chicago Defender*, in *ibid.*, 410. He also said that he was in New Orleans at the Temple Theater, which opened in 1909. He may have conflated a number of visits into one event, or perhaps it was a different theater. Whichever is the case, the contemporaneous reports are usually more reliable than memory.

88. I have attempted to find out who holds the copyright for "Mamie's Blues." The Roy J Carew Co. (Tempo Music) do not know. Morton's legal representative, Thomas M. Hunt, has not responded to enquiries. Universal Music directed me to Hal Leonard, who handle their licenses. Hal Leonard do not hold the rights. Part of the explanation may be contained in a letter Morton sent to Roy Carew on December 23, 1939. "Mamie Desdume, wrote Mamie's Blues in the late 90's. I don't like to take credit for something that don't belong to me. I guess she's dead by now, and there would probably be no royalty to pay, but she did write it." Folder 105, MSS 507 (New Orleans: Williams Research Center, Historic New Orleans Collection).

89. The only exception to this is the ascending mode of the melodic minor scale. As the name suggests this scale is not used for harmonic purposes in European tonal music. Later jazz musicians do use this scale harmonically in relation to altered harmony. See Mark Levin, *The Jazz Theory Book* (Petaluma, CA: Sher Music, 1995). Bunk Johnson also recorded a version of the "219 Blues" in 1944 while in San Francisco with the Yerba Buena Jazz Band. The band members were keen New Orleans revivalists who would not play any tune written after 1929.

CHAPTER 6

1. Anthony Maggio, "The Birth of the Blues," *The Overture* 35, no. 9 (1955) (The Professional Musicians, Local 47 Archives Department). My thanks to Lawrence Gushee for passing this on to me.

2. *Ibid.*

3. This tune was issued in sheet music and on piano roll. "I Got De Blues," by Chris Smith & Eugene Bowman, Music for the Aeolian Grand (piano roll) 40898 (1906). Chris

Smith went on to have his biggest hit in 1914 with "Ballin' the Jack," which was co-written with Jim Burris and starting a dance craze that lasted a decade.

4. Jelly Roll Morton, *Down Beat*, September 1938, 4 (Performing Arts Reading Room, Library of Congress).

5. "Oh Ain't I Got the Blues" (1871), by A. A. Chapman, published by J. W. Smith Jr. in Fulton Street, New York (Performing Arts Reading Room, Library of Congress).

6. "I Have Got the Blues To Day" (1850), by Miss Sarah M. Graham & Gustave Blessner, published by Firth Pond & Co., New York (Duke University Library, Historic American Sheet Music 1850–1920). For further information on early blues titles, see Peter C. Muir, *Long Lost Blues: Popular Blues in America, 1850–1920* (Chicago: University of Illinois Press, 2010).

7. Leon Jean Barzin is recorded in the 1910 census for New Orleans. Both he and his more famous son, Leon Eugene Barzin, played viola with Toscanini at the Met. It seems that Maggio made little effort to exploit his position as a pioneer in the publication of the blues, although he did write another twelve-bar tune in 1910. "Bad Rag" was not published; the only known copy is a manuscript in the Music Division of the Library of Congress. Muir, "Before 'Crazy Blues': Commercial Blues in America 1850–1920," 311.

8. Hughey Cannon and John Queen, "Just Because She Made Dem Goo-Goo Eyes" (1900) (Performing Arts Reading Room, Library of Congress).

9. "Tom the Tattler," *Indianapolis Freeman*, May 25, 1901; Abbott and Seroff, *Ragged but Right: Black Travelling Shows, "Coon Songs," and the Dark Pathway to Blues and Jazz*, 13.

10. His brother, Louis, said of "Goo-Goo Eyes," "Freddie used to play all them old things." Louis Keppard, "Interview Summary, January 19, 1961," ed. Richard B. Allen, William Russell, and Ralph Collins (New Orleans: William Ransom Hogan Jazz Archive, Tulane University). The Keppard family lived on the downtown side of Canal Street, north of Basin Street, but according to Lawrence Gushee, Keppard "can't be identified as 'Creole,' in the sense of having been brought up in close contact with French language and culture." Lawrence Gushee, *The Story of the Creole Band* (Oxford: Oxford University Press, 2005), 47–48.

11. David Chevan, "Written Music in Early Jazz" (diss., City University of New York, 1997), 166–79. Chevan argues that the arrangement was probably derived from the piano sheet music.

12. Tim Brooks, *Lost Sounds: Blacks and the Birth of the Recording Industry, 1890–1919* (Urbana and Chicago: University of Illinois Press, 2004), 410; Handy, *Father of the Blues*, 11.

13. Handy, *Father of the Blues*, 142–43.

14. The opening chorus is arranged for a quartet; subsequent choruses are arranged for instruments.

15. W. C. Handy, interviewed by Alan Lomax, Washington, D.C., May 1938 (Library of Congress, AFC 1621 A3 and B1).

16. W. C. Handy, "How I Came to Write the 'Memphis Blues,'" *New York Age*, December 7, 1916. My thanks to Lynn Abbott for passing on this newspaper article to me. "Spanish tuning" usually refers to an open G tuning. Evans, *Big Road Blues*, 209. The term probably derives from Henry Worrall's "Spanish Fandango" (1860), which was published with open G tuning. jasobrecht.com/blues-origins-spanish-fandango-and-sebastopol/ (Accessed April 20, 2012).

17. Handy, *Father of the Blues*, 74.

18. *Ibid.*, 120.

19. Averill, *Four Parts, No Waiting*, 163.

20. Muir, *Long Lost Blues*, 115.

21. Transposed from the original key of G. Adapted from *ibid.*, 115.

22. Handy, *Father of the Blues*, 28.

23. *Ibid.*, 142.

24. *Ibid.*

25. *Ibid.*

26. Alphonse Picou showed a copy of his baptismal certificate to Robert Goffin. His certificate stated: "In the year 1879, on February 9th, I undersigned vicar of the Church St Augustin baptized Florestan Alphonse Picou, born on October 19th, 1878, son of Alfred Picou and Clothilde Marie Serpas." October 1879 is given on the 1900 (Twelfth) Federal Census of the United States, Ward 5, District 49, sheet 10. His date of birth given to the WWI Registration Board was October 19, 1879. The Louisiana Birth Record Index 1790–1899, Vol. 73, page 269, records October 19, 1878 (Ancestry.com).

27. 1880 Federal Census of the United States, Parish of Orleans, Enumeration District 49, sheet 45 (Ancestry.com), gives the family home as 46 Kerlerec Street. Alphonse Picou gave two different streets in which he believed he was born, saying Bayou Road to Robert Goffin and Hospital Street (renamed Governor Nicholls Street in 1911), between Liberty and St. Claude in the Sixth Ward, in his interviews for the Hogan Jazz Archive. The family lived at 56 Kerlerec Street, according to the street numbers given in Soards' New Orleans City Directory 1892, 647; Soards' New Orleans City Directory 1893, 679.

28. She resided in 1892 at 492 ½ St. Claude Street, where she took in "washing."

29. Alphonse Picou is recorded as a "tinsmith" resident at 727 North Robertson Street in the 1898 city directory, and at 827 Robertson Street in the 1900 census.

30. Goffin, *La Nouvelle-Orléans Capital Du Jazz*.

31. www.hurricanebrassband.nl/Brassband%20excelsior%20brass%20band.htm (accessed January 14, 2011).

32. William "Baba" Ridgley, "Interview Summary, April 11, 1961," ed. John Handy, Richard B. Allen, and Marjorie T. Zander (New Orleans: William Ransom Hogan Jazz Archive, Tulane University).

33. Alex Bigard, "Interview Digest April 30, 1960," ed. Ralph Collins, William Russell, and Richard B. Allen (New Orleans: William Ransom Hogan Jazz Archive, Tulane University).

34. Maurice Durand, "Interview Summary, August 22, 1958," ed. William Russell (New Orleans: William Ransom Hogan Jazz Archive, Tulane University); Hypolite Charles, "Interview Digest, April 13, 1963," ed. Richard B. Allen (New Orleans: William Ransom Hogan Jazz Archive, Tulane University).

35. Amos M. White, "Interview Digest, August 23, 1958," ed. William Russell (New Orleans: William Ransom Hogan Jazz Archive, Tulane University).

36. Goffin, *La Nouvelle-Orléans Capital Du Jazz*, 123 (my translation).

37. "New Hopes Hall" in the *Jazzmen* interviews.

38. Alphonse Picou, "Interview Transcript, April 4, 1958, 'Picou,' Folder 3," in MSS 536, ed. William Russell, Al Rose, and Ralph Collins (New Orleans: Williams Research Center, Historic New Orleans Collection).

39. Goffin, *La Nouvelle-Orléans Capital Du Jazz*, 123–24.

40. *Ibid.*, 124.

41. Bechet et al., "Interview Digest, June 1944 & November 19, 1945."

42. Lomax, *Mister Jelly Roll*, 72.

43. *Ibid.*, 72. I have not been able to check the accuracy of this with the original interview notes in the American Folklife Collection of the Library of Congress.

44. Picou, "Interview Transcript, April 4, 1958, 'Picou,' Folder 3."

45. *Ibid.*

46. Joseph M. Daly, "Chicken Reel, or, Performer's Buck" (Boston: Daly Music Publishing, 1910) (University of Colorado Digital Sheet Music Collection).

47. There were a good number of "Chicken" songs to appear around the turn of the century, including "Chicken Don't Roost Too High" (1899) and "Dat's the Way to Spell Chicken" (1902).

48. Rose and Souchon, *New Orleans Jazz*, 44.

49. *Ibid.*, 44.

50. George "Pops" Foster, "Interview (Digest), Reel B Track 2, 1969," ed. Tom Stoddard (New Orleans: William Ransom Hogan Jazz Archive, Tulane University). This is from the audio tape rather than the digest.

51. Picou, "Interview Transcript, April 4, 1958, 'Picou,' Folder 3," in MSS 536 (New Orleans: Williams Research Center, Historic New Orleans Collection).

52. Alphonse Picou, "*Jazzmen* Interviews, Box 16 C," in MSS 559 (New Orleans: Williams Research Center, Historic New Orleans Collection).

53. Having listened to the recording, I am reasonably certain that Picou said "one man" and not "one band" as suggested in the Hogan Archive transcript.

54. Picou, "Interview Transcript, April 4, 1958, 'Picou,' Folder 3," in MSS 536 (New Orleans: Williams Research Center, Historic New Orleans Collection). This is a composite of the transcript and the recording.

55. Alphonse Picou, "The Story of 'Coon Blues,'" *Transcript of the 1938 Library of Congress Recordings of Jelly Roll Morton*, 158.

56. Picou, "Interview Transcript, April 4, 1958, 'Picou,' Folder 3," in MSS 536 (New Orleans: Williams Research Center, Historic New Orleans Collection).

57. Goffin, *La Nouvelle-Orléans Capital Du Jazz*, 125–26.

58. Sidney Bechet, *Treat It Gentle* (London: Jazz Book Club Edition, Cassell, 1962), 64; Joshua Berrett, "Louis Armstrong and Opera," *Musical Quarterly* 76, no. 2 (1992): 227.

59. Transposed from G major; Spaeth, *Barber Shop Ballads and How to Sing Them*, 14. It will be seen that in these endings the bass voice stays on its original note and consequently these chords are inverted, meaning they have a note other than the root of the chord in the bass voice.

60. Alphonse Picou, "High Society," transcribed by Lloyd Miller, *Jazz Trough the Ages* 4 (Eastern Arts) (New Orleans: William Ransom Hogan Jazz Archive, Tulane University).

CHAPTER 7

1. *Variety*, October 19, 1917; Koenig, *Evolution of Ragtime & Blues to Jazz*, 126–27.

2. Rose and Souchon, *New Orleans Jazz*, 94.

3. *Ibid.*, 76.

4. Dominick James ("Nick") LaRocca, "Interview June 2, 1958" (New Orleans: William Ransom Hogan Jazz Archive, Tulane University).

5. Nick LaRocca, "Interview May 21, 1958" (New Orleans: William Ransom Hogan Jazz Archive, Tulane University).

6. I have transposed this from E♭ as it is in the piano sheet music.

7. LaRocca, "Interview May 21, 1958."

8. Maggio, "The Birth of the Blues"; Abbott and Seroff, "'They Cert'ly Sound Good to Me': Sheet Music, Southern Vaudeville, and the Commercial Ascendancy of the Blues," 406.

9. Ray Lopez, "Interview Digest, August 30, 1958," ed. William Russell (New Orleans: William Ransom Hogan Jazz Archive, Tulane University).

10. Marquis, *In Search of Buddy Bolden*, 22; Rose and Souchon, *New Orleans Jazz*, 116.

11. Dominick James ("Nick") LaRocca, "Interview June 9, 1959" (New Orleans: William Ransom Hogan Jazz Archive, Tulane University).

12. This is in the key of F.

13. Abbott, "'Play That Barber Shop Chord': A Case for the African-American Origin of Barbershop Harmony," 308.

14. Spaeth, *Barber Shop Ballads and How to Sing Them*, 18.

15. *Ibid.*, 18.

16. *Ibid.*, 19.

17. Rudi Blesh, *Shining Trumpets: A History of Jazz* (London: Cassell, 1954), 106.

18. Samuel A. Floyd and Marsha J. Reisser, "The Sources and Resources of Classic Ragtime Music," *Black Music Research Journal* 4 (1984): 30.

19. Winthrop Sargeant, *Jazz: Hot and Hybrid* (Da Capo Paperback, 1938; reprint, 1976), 151.

20. Henry Edward Krehbiel, *Afro-American Folksong: A Study in Racial and National Music* (New York and London: G. Schirmer, 1914), 43.

21. LaRocca, "Interview June 2, 1958."

22. LaRocca, "Interview May 21, 1958."

23. Dominick James ("Nick") LaRocca, "Interview October 26, 1959" (New Orleans: William Ransom Hogan Jazz Archive, Tulane University).

24. David Sager, sleeve notes to King Oliver, *Off the Record: The Complete 1923 Jazz Band Recordings* (Archeophone Records, 2006).

25. George Brunies, "Interview Transcript, June 3, 1958," ed. William Russell (New Orleans: William Ransom Hogan Jazz Archive, Tulane University).

26. "Papa" Jack Laine, "Interview Transcript, April 21, 1951," ed. Edmund Souchon (New Orleans: William Ransom Hogan Jazz Archive, Tulane University).

27. "Papa" Jack Laine, "Interview Transcript, March 26, 1957," ed. William Russell and Richard B. Allen (New Orleans: William Ransom Hogan Jazz Archive, Tulane University).

28. "Papa" Jack Laine, "Interview Digest, April 25, 1964," ed. Richard B. Allen and Bill Stuckey (New Orleans: William Ransom Hogan Jazz Archive, Tulane University).

29. "Papa" Jack Laine, "Interview Digest, February 27, 1959," ed. Johnny Wiggs, Edmond Souchon, Raymond Burke, Jake Scaimbra, William Russell, Richard B. Allen, and Paul R. Crawford (New Orleans: William Ransom Hogan Jazz Archive, Tulane University).

30. Laine, "Interview Digest, April 25, 1964."

31. Laine, "Interview Transcript, March 26, 1957."

32. *Ibid.*

33. "Papa" Jack Laine, "Interview Digest, May 23, 1960," ed. William Russell, Ralph Collins, and Marjorie Zander (New Orleans: William Ransom Hogan Jazz Archive, Tulane University).

34. The tune was a standard of New Orleans bands revivalists. It was also adapted to become "Donna Lee" by Charlie Parker and Miles Davis.

35. For differing views on this, see James Earl Henry, "The Origins of Barbershop Harmony: A Study of Barbershop's Musical Link to Other African American Musics as Evidenced through Recordings and Arrangements of Early Black and White Quartets" (diss., Washington University, 2000); Peter Van Der Merwe, *Origins of the Popular Style* (Oxford: Clarendon Press, 1989).

36. Spaeth, *Barber Shop Ballads and How to Sing Them*, 17.

CHAPTER 8

1. Goffin, *La Nouvelle-Orléans Capital Du Jazz*, 50.

2. *Ibid.*, 52.

3. Goffin consistently spells Galloway as Gallaway. I have silently corrected throughout.

4. Goffin, *La Nouvelle-Orléans Capital Du Jazz*, 52.

5. *Ibid.*, 53.

6. *Ibid.*, 54.

7. *Ibid.*, 131.

8. *Ibid.*, 136.

9. *Ibid.*, 137.

10. *Ibid.*, 90.

11. Goffin spelled the name of the banjo player as Jim Gibbson.

12. Goffin, *La Nouvelle-Orléans Capital Du Jazz*, 91.

13. *Ibid.*, 92.

14. *Ibid.*, 93.

15. *Ibid.*, 92.

16. *Ibid.*, 98.

17. *Ibid.*

18. Cornish, "*Jazzmen* Interviews, Box 16 C."

19. Emile Barnes, "Interview Digest, December 20, 1960," ed. William Russell and Ralph Collins (New Orleans: William Ransom Hogan Jazz Archive, Tulane University). According to David Evans, "Clarinet and second violin are more or less interchangeable in European and Euro-American 'string' bands and other dance ensembles."

20. Joseph, "Interview Transcript November 26, 1958."

21. Eddie "Montudi" Garland, "Interview Transcript, April 20, 1971," ed. Richard B. Allen and Floyd Levin (New Orleans: William Ransom Hogan Jazz Archive, Tulane University).

22. Bocage, "Interview Digest, February 5, 1962."

23. Lawrence Duhé, "Interview Transcript, June 9, 1957, Wellman Braud & Charles Devore," ed. William Russell and Richard B. Allen (New Orleans: William Ransom Hogan Jazz Archive, Tulane University).

24. *Ibid.*

25. Peter Bocage, "Interview Transcript, January 29, 1959," ed. Richard B. Allen and William Russell (New Orleans: William Ransom Hogan Jazz Archive, Tulane University).

26. Goffin, *La Nouvelle-Orléans Capital Du Jazz*, 133.

27. Fewclothes Cabaret was between Basin Street and Canal and Customhouse (Iberville). Rose and Souchon, *New Orleans Jazz*, 224. The 1906 Soards' City Directory includes among "Lunch Houses" "Foucault, George, 135 N Basin." In the 1910 census George

Foucault "white" is at the same address and operated a saloon (Thirteenth Census of the United States, New Orleans, Precinct 2, District 58, Sheet 4A).

28. Goffin, *La Nouvelle-Orléans Capital Du Jazz*, 133.

29. Bocage, "Interview Transcript, January 29, 1959."

30. Louis Keppard, "Interview Summary, January 19, 1961," ed. Richard B. Allen, William Russell, and Ralph Collins (New Orleans: William Ransom Hogan Jazz Archive, Tulane University).

31. Goffin, *La Nouvelle-Orléans Capital Du Jazz*, 70.

32. *Ibid.*, 136.

33. *Ibid.*, 69.

34. *Ibid.*, 134.

35. *Ibid.*, 72.

36. *Ibid.*, 73.

37. Rose and Souchon, *New Orleans Jazz*, 97.

38. Alcide "Slow Drag" Pavageau, "Interview Transcript, December 10, 1958" (New Orleans: William Ransom Hogan Jazz Archive, Tulane University).

39. Bocage, "Interview Transcript, January 29, 1959."

40. Goffin, *La Nouvelle-Orléans Capital Du Jazz*, 132; Rose and Souchon, *New Orleans Jazz*, 45.

41. Rose and Souchon, *New Orleans Jazz*, 80.

42. *Ibid.*, 29.

43. Blesh, *Shining Trumpets*, 156, 81; Thomas Brothers, "Who's on First, What's Second, and Where Did They Come From? The Social and Musical Textures of Early Jazz," in *Early Twentieth Century Brass Idioms: Art, Jazz, and Other Popular Traditions*, ed. Howard T. Weiner, *Studies in Jazz*, No. 58 (Lanham, MD: Scarecrow Press, 2009), 17.

44. Cornish, "*Jazzmen* Interviews, Box 16 C."

45. Letter from Bunk Johnson to Roy Carew, Blesh and Janis, *They All Played Ragtime*, 170; Karl Gert zur Heide, "Who Was the Leader of Charles Bolden's Orchestra?" *New Orleans Music* 5, no. 2 (1994): 8.

46. Samuel B. Charters, *Jazz: New Orleans 1885–1957* (Stanhope, NJ: Walter C. Allen, 1958), 53; Karl Gert zur Heide, "Who Was the Leader of Charles Bolden's Orchestra?" 8. The following is an extract from the notes of an interview with Paul Beaulieu that gives further information about the Bloom Philharmonic Orchestra:

> Mr. Bloom, a flutist, worked for L. Frank and Company, taking care of their livestock; Bloom studied with Louis Tio. PB played cello in the same orchestra with Bloom. Louis Tio was the conductor. There were six first violins; four second violins; one viola; one cello; two basses; flute; two clarinets, [et al?]. Charles Elgar was concertmaster; some others: Armand Piron, [Ferdinand] Valteau, [John Tateneau?], Anatole Victor, Vincent Roberts, Mr. Leclair, Dee Dee Brooks, Etienne Nickolas [spelling?] (a viola player who at one time lived around the corner [from PB], and has been dead [for quite some years?]; PB played cello; [Paul?] Dominguez played bass.

Paul Beaulieu, "Interview Summary, June 11, 1960" (New Orleans: William Ransom Hogan Jazz Archive, Tulane University).

47. Barnes, "Interview Digest, December 20, 1960."

48. There is some doubt about whether Warner or Lewis is the person holding the C clarinet in the photograph; Ashforth, "The Bolden Photo—One More Time." The same question is taken up by Karl Gert zur Heide, "Who Was the Leader of Charles Bolden's Orchestra?" My own view is that Warner (standing) is posing with an A clarinet, which is longer than the B♭ clarinet of Frank Lewis (seated). Hobson, "Buddy Bolden's Blues."

49. Marquis, *In Search of Buddy Bolden*, 82.

50. Manuel Manetta, "Interview Digest March 21, 1957," ed. Nesuhi Ertegun, William Russell, Richard B. Allen, and Robert Campbell (New Orleans: William Ransom Hogan Jazz Archive, Tulane University).

51. Willie E. Humphrey (the elder) and Willie J. Humphrey (the younger), "Interview Digest, March 15, 1959," ed. William Russell and Ralph Collins (New Orleans: William Ransom Hogan Jazz Archive, Tulane University).

52. Karl Koenig, *The Plantation Belt: The Musical History of Plaquemines Parish, Louisiana* (Running Springs, CA: Basin Street Books, undated), 1–3.

53. Cornish, "*Jazzmen* Interviews, Box 16 C."

54. [*Sic*].

55. Bella Cornish, "Interview Transcript January 13, 1959," ed. William Russell (New Orleans: William Ransom Hogan Jazz Archive, Tulane University).

56. Goffin, *La Nouvelle-Orléans Capital Du Jazz*, 80.

57. Rose and Souchon, *New Orleans Jazz*, 99.

58. Bocage, "Interview Digest, February 5, 1962."

59. Bocage, "Interview Transcript, January 29, 1959."

60. Octave Crosby, "Interview Summary, March 26, 1959" (New Orleans: William Ransom Hogan Jazz Archive, Tulane University).

61. *Ibid.*

62. Alfred Williams, "Interview Summary, April 30, 1960" (New Orleans: William Ransom Hogan Jazz Archive, Tulane University).

63. Charlie Love, "Interview Transcript, June 20, 1958" (New Orleans: William Ransom Hogan Jazz Archive, Tulane University).

64. Andy Ridley interview with Louis Keppard, quoted in Andy Ridley, *I'm Just a Plain Ordinary Guitar Player . . . But I'll Scare the Best of Them: The Autobiography of Louis Keppard*, unpublished manuscript, 1985; Abbott, "'Play That Barber Shop Chord': A Case for the African-American Origin of Barbershop Harmony," 318; *ibid.*

65. Johnson and Johnson, *The Books of American Negro Spirituals*, 36.

66. Rose and Souchon, *New Orleans Jazz*, 120.

67. Kid Thomas Valentine, "Interview Summary, November 8, 1959" (New Orleans: William Ransom Hogan Jazz Archive, Tulane University).

68. Kid Thomas Valentine, "Interview Digest, March 22, 1957 (for *Life Magazine*)," ed. William Russell and Nesuhi Ertegun (New Orleans: William Ransom Hogan Jazz Archive, Tulane University).

69. Rose and Souchon, *New Orleans Jazz: A Family Album*, 3.

70. Ricard Alexis, "Interview Summary, January 16, 1959" (New Orleans: William Ransom Hogan Jazz Archive, Tulane University).

71. *Ibid.*

72. Lee Collins, "Interview Transcript, June 2, 1958" (New Orleans: William Ransom Hogan Jazz Archive, Tulane University).

73. Bocage, "Interview Transcript, January 29, 1959."

74. Bunk Johnson, "Folder 141," in MSS 512 (New Orleans: Williams Research Center, Historic New Orleans Collection).

75. Alexis, "Interview Summary, January 16, 1959."

76. Punch Miller, "Interview Digest, August 20, 1959," ed. Richard B. Allen (New Orleans: William Ransom Hogan Jazz Archive, Tulane University).

77. Punch Miller (Earnest Burden) registered for the draft at Raceland on June 5, 1917, giving his date of birth as May 10, 1894. His "age in years" is accordingly given as 23 (Ancestry.com).

78. Hobson, "New Orleans Jazz and the Blues."

79. Ernest Punch Miller, "Interview Digest April 4, 1960," ed. Paul R. Crawford, Richard B. Allen, and Lionel Robinson (New Orleans: William Ransom Hogan Jazz Archive, Tulane University). Punch only played the first four bars of the melody, so I have completed the phrase with Johnny Dodds's lead from King Oliver's Jazz Band, "High Society Rag," Okeh 4933 (Chicago, June 22, 1923).

80. There is theoretically a clash of harmony when Petit's line plays an A-natural against the B♭ (standard changes) chord in (m. 7). To my ears the A-natural is preferable to the more theoretically "correct" B♭.

81. Punch Miller, April 4, 1960, Transcribed from the Audio Tape (New Orleans: William Ransom Hogan Jazz Archive, Tulane University).

82. Clarence "Little Dad" Vincent, "Interview Digest, December 3, 1959," ed. Richard B. Allen (New Orleans: William Ransom Hogan Jazz Archive, Tulane University).

83. Louis Armstrong in Hugues Panassié, *Louis Armstrong* (Da Capo, 1971), 51.

84. Steve Angrum, "Interview Digest, August 8, 1961," ed. William Russell and Ralph Collins (New Orleans: William Ransom Hogan Jazz Archive, Tulane University).

85. Bocage, "Interview Transcript, January 29, 1959."

86. Schuller, *Early Jazz*, 85–86.

87. Larry Gushee, "King Oliver's Creole Jazz Band," in Martin Williams, *The Art of Jazz: Ragtime to Be-Bop* (New York: Da Capo, 1981), 46.

88. Edward Brooks, *The Young Louis Armstrong on Record: A Critical Survey of the Early Recordings, 1923–1928* (Lanham, MD: Scarecrow Press, 2002), 14.

89. Samuel Charters, *A Trumpet around the Corner: The Story of New Orleans Jazz* (Jackson: University Press of Mississippi, 2008), 176.

90. "Market Street Blues," OK 8201, St. Louis, ca. December 2, 1924, Rust, *Jazz Records 1897–1942*; Charters, *A Trumpet around the Corner*, 176.

91. Ken Burns and Lynn Norvick, *Jazz* (London: BBC, 2001).

92. Robert Gottlieb, *Reading Jazz* (New York: Vintage, 1996), 746.

93. Bocage, "Interview Transcript, January 29, 1959."

94. Bechet, *Treat It Gentle*, 91–92; Abbott, "'Play That Barber Shop Chord,'" 315.

95. Johnny St. Cyr, "Interview Digest, August 27, 1958," ed. William Russell (New Orleans: William Ransom Hogan Jazz Archive, Tulane University).

96. It could be that this solo was a reference to "Dipper Mouth Blues" (1923). The solo is similar to a countermelody that Armstrong played.

97. It is not certain that Johnny St. Cyr on banjo was playing a G7. It could be that he was playing an A diminished chord. One possible explanation for the notes that Armstrong played is that this is an example of the D7 (omit 3) cadence (ending number 6, example 29). Note how the D in measure 9 becomes E♭ in measure 10 before resolving to

E-natural at the end of measure 11. This is consistent with tenor voice leading. The A in measure 9 is the baritone voice, which descends back to G in the final measure.

98. Peter Ecklund, *Great Trumpet Solos of Louis Armstrong* (New York: Chas. Colin Publications, undated), 42, 61.

99. Armstrong, *Satchmo*, 35; Abbott, "'Play That Barber Shop Chord,'" 318.

100. Louis Armstrong, interview with Richard Hadlock, Joshua Berrett, "Louis Armstrong and Opera," *Musical Quarterly* 76, no. 2: 218.

CHAPTER 9

1. Burns and Norvick, *Jazz.*

2. Paul Oliver, "That Certain Feeling: Blues and Jazz . . . In 1890?" *Popular Music* 10, no. 1 (1991): 18.

3. Lynn Abbott in Will Buckingham, "Louis Armstrong and the Waifs' Home," *The Jazz Archivist: A Newsletter of the William Ransom Hogan Jazz Archive* XXIV (2011): 8.

4. Ory, "Interview Transcript, April 20, 1957 (for *Life Magazine*)." Ory was asked by Nesuhi Ertegun whether Galloway's band was "more like a jazz band (in relation to Peyton's band)." Ory replied, "Yeah."

5. *Ibid.*

6. Joseph, "Interview Transcript November 26, 1958."

BIBLIOGRAPHY

Abbott, Lynn. "'Play That Barber Shop Chord': A Case for the African-American Origin of Barbershop Harmony." *American Music* 10, no. 3 (1992): 289–325.

———. "Remembering Mr. E. Belfield Spriggins: First Man of Jazzology." *78 Quarterly* 1, no. 10: 13–51.

———. "'A Worthy Copy of the Subject He Mimics'. Ben Harney in Context, 1896–1898." *Rag-Time Ephemeralist*, no. 3 (2002): 42–47.

Abbott, Lynn, and Doug Seroff. *Out of Sight: The Rise of African American Popular Music 1889–1895*. Jackson: University Press of Mississippi, 2002.

———. *Ragged but Right: Black Travelling Shows, "Coon Songs," and the Dark Pathway to Blues and Jazz*. Jackson: University Press of Mississippi, 2007.

———. "'They Cert'ly Sound Good to Me': Sheet Music, Southern Vaudeville, and the Commercial Ascendancy of the Blues." *American Music* 14, no. 4 (1996): 402–54.

Alexis, Ricard. "Interview Summary, January 16, 1959." New Orleans: William Ransom Hogan Jazz Archive, Tulane University.

Allen, William Francis, Charles Pickard Ware, and Lucy McKim Garrison. *Slave Songs of the United States*. New York: Dover, 1867. Reprint, 1995.

Angrum, Steve. "Interview Digest, August 8, 1961," ed. William Russell and Ralph Collins. New Orleans: William Ransom Hogan Jazz Archive, Tulane University.

Armstrong, Louis. *Satchmo: My Life in New Orleans*. Peter Davies, 1955; reprint, Sedgwick and Jackson, 1957.

Ashforth, Alden. "The Bolden Photo—One More Time." *Annual Review of Jazz Studies* 3 (1985).

Averill, Gage. *Four Parts, No Waiting: A Social History of Barbershop Harmony*. New York: Oxford University Press, 2003.

Barker, Danny, and Alyn Shipton. *Buddy Bolden and the Last Days of Storyville*. London and New York: Cassell, 1998.

Barnes, Emile. "Interview Digest, December 20, 1960," ed. William Russell and Ralph Collins. New Orleans: William Ransom Hogan Jazz Archive, Tulane University.

Beaulieu, Paul. "Interview Summary, June 11, 1960." New Orleans: William Ransom Hogan Jazz Archive, Tulane University.

Bechet, Sidney. *Treat It Gentle*. London: Jazz Book Club Edition, Cassell, 1962.

Bechet, Sidney, and Manuel Perez et al. "Interview Digest, June 1944 & November 19, 1945," ed. John Reid and Richard B. Allen. New Orleans: William Ransom Hogan Jazz Archive, Tulane University.

Berlin, Edward A. *King of Ragtime: Scott Joplin and His Era*. New York and Oxford: Oxford University Press, 1994.

Berrett, Joshua. "Louis Armstrong and Opera." *Musical Quarterly* 76, no. 2: 216–41.

Bigard, Alex. "Interview Digest April 30, 1960," ed. Ralph Collins, William Russell, and Richard B. Allen. New Orleans: William Ransom Hogan Jazz Archive, Tulane University.

Blesh, Rudi. *Shining Trumpets: A History of Jazz.* London: Cassell, 1954.

Blesh, Rudi, and Harriet Janis. *They All Played Ragtime: The True Story of an American Music.* London: Sedgwick and Jackson, 1950. Reprint, 1960.

Bocage, Peter. "Interview Digest, February 5, 1962," ed. Barry Martyn and Richard Knowles. New Orleans: William Ransom Hogan Jazz Archive, Tulane University.

Bocage, Peter. "Interview Transcript, January 29, 1959," ed. Richard B. Allen and William Russell. New Orleans: William Ransom Hogan Jazz Archive, Tulane University.

Bowers, Jane, and William Westcott. "Mama Yancey and the Revival Blues Tradition." *Black Music Research Journal* 12, no. 2 (1992): 171–213.

Bradford, Perry. *Born with the Blues.* New York: Oak Publications, 1965.

Brooks, Edward. *The Young Louis Armstrong on Record: A Critical Survey of the Early Recordings, 1923–1928.* Lanham, MD: Scarecrow Press, 2002.

Brooks, Tim. *Lost Sounds: Blacks and the Birth of the Recording Industry, 1890–1919.* Urbana and Chicago: University of Illinois Press, 2004.

Brothers, Thomas. "Who's on First, What's Second, and Where Did They Come From? The Social and Musical Textures of Early Jazz." In *Early Twentieth Century Brass Idioms: Art, Jazz, and Other Popular Traditions,* ed. Howard T. Weiner. Lanham, MD: Scarecrow Press, 2009.

Brown, Steve. "Interview Transcript, April 22, 1958," ed. Richard Allen and William Russell. New Orleans: William Ransom Hogan Jazz Archive, Tulane University.

Brunies, George. "Interview Transcript, June 3, 1958," ed. William Russell. New Orleans: William Ransom Hogan Jazz Archive, Tulane University.

Buckingham, Will. "Louis Armstrong and the Waifs' Home." *The Jazz Archivist: A Newsletter of the William Ransom Hogan Jazz Archive* XXIV (2011): 2–15.

Burns, Ken, and Lynn Norvick. *Jazz.* London: BBC, 2001.

Calt, Stephen. *I'd Rather Be the Devil: Skip James and the Blues.* New York: Da Capo, 1994.

Castle, Mr. and Mrs. Vernon. *Modern Dancing.* New York: Harper & Row, 1914; reprint, New York: Da Capo, 1980.

Charles, Hypolite. "Interview Digest, April 13, 1963," ed. Richard B. Allen. New Orleans: William Ransom Hogan Jazz Archive, Tulane University.

Charters, Samuel B. *Jazz: New Orleans 1885-1957.* Stanhope NJ: Walter C. Allen, 1958.

———. *A Trumpet around the Corner: The Story of New Orleans Jazz.* Jackson: University Press of Mississippi, 2008.

Chevan, David. "Written Music in Early Jazz." Diss., City University of New York, 1997.

Clementin, Ferrand. "Interview Digest August 2, 1973," ed. Richard B. Allen. New Orleans: William Ransom Hogan Jazz Archive, Tulane University.

Clementine, Ferrand and Mathilda. "Interview Digest, November 29, 1974, Box 5 B." In MSS 559. New Orleans: Williams Research Center, Historic New Orleans Collection.

Collins, Lee. "Interview Transcript, June 2, 1958." New Orleans: William Ransom Hogan Jazz Archive, Tulane University.

———. *Oh, Didn't He Ramble: The Life Story of Lee Collins.* Ed. Mary Collins. Urbana: University of Illinois Press, 1974.

Cornish, Bella. "Interview Transcript January 13, 1959," ed. William Russell. New Orleans: William Ransom Hogan Jazz Archive.

Cornish, Willy. *"Jazzmen Interviews, Box 16 C."* In MSS 559. New Orleans: Williams Research Center, Historic New Orleans Collection.

Crosby, Octave. "Interview Summary, March 26, 1959." New Orleans: William Ransom Hogan Jazz Archive, Tulane University.

Dawson, Eddie. "Interview Digest April 5, 1972," ed. Richard B. Allen. New Orleans: William Ransom Hogan Jazz Archive, Tulane University.

———. "Interview Digest August 11, 1959," ed. William Russell and Ralph Collins. New Orleans: William Ransom Hogan Jazz Archive, Tulane University.

———. "Interview Digest June 28, 1961," ed. William Russell and Ralph Collins. New Orleans: William Ransom Hogan Jazz Archive, Tulane University.

Delaunay, Charles, and Ian Munro Smyth. *Hot Discography*. Paris: Hot Jazz, 1936.

Desdunes, Rodolphe Lucien. *Our People and Our History: Fifty Creole Portraits*. Translated by Sister Dorothea Olga McCants. Baton Rouge: Louisiana State University Press, 1911; reprint, 1973.

Dodds, Baby, and Larry Gara. *The Baby Dodds Story*, rev. ed. Baton Rouge: Louisiana State University Press, 1992.

Duhé, Lawrence. "Interview Digest, 1960," ed. George Brown. New Orleans: William Ransom Hogan Jazz Archive, Tulane University.

———. "Interview Transcript, June 9, 1957, Wellman Braud & Charles Devore," ed. William Russell and Richard B. Allen. New Orleans: William Ransom Hogan Jazz Archive, Tulane University.

Durand, Maurice. "Interview Summary, August 22, 1958," ed. William Russell. New Orleans: William Ransom Hogan Jazz Archive, Tulane University.

Ecklund, Peter. *Great Trumpet Solos of Louis Armstrong*. New York: Chas. Colin Publications, undated.

Evans, David. *Big Road Blues: Tradition and Creativity in the Folk Blues*. New York: Da Capo, 1982; reprint, 1987.

Farr, Susie. "Interview Notes, July 25, 1967," ed. Richard Allen. New Orleans: The William Ransom Hogan Jazz Archive, Tulane University.

Floyd, Samuel A., and Marsha J. Reisser. "The Sources and Resources of Classic Ragtime Music." *Black Music Research Journal* 4 (1984): 22–59.

Fogarty, Joseph E. "Interview Transcript June 18, 1969," ed. William Russell and William Hogan. New Orleans: William Ransom Hogan Jazz Archive, Tulane University.

Foster, George "Pops." "Interview (Digest), Reel B Track 2, 1969," ed. Tom Stoddard. New Orleans: William Ransom Hogan Jazz Archive, Tulane University.

French, Morris. "Interview Digest, June 24, 1960," ed. Richard B. Allen and Marjorie T. Zander. New Orleans: William Ransom Hogan Jazz Archive, Tulane University.

Garland, Eddie. "Interview Digest August 8, 1958," ed. William Russell. New Orleans: William Ransom Hogan Jazz Archive, Tulane University.

Garland, Eddie "Montudi." "Interview Transcript, April 20, 1971," ed. Richard B. Allen and Floyd Levin. New Orleans: William Ransom Hogan Jazz Archive, Tulane University.

Gert zur Heide, Karl. "Who Was the Leader of Charles Bolden's Orchestra?" *New Orleans Music* 5, no. 2 (1994): 6–10.

Glenny, Albert. "Interview Transcript, March 27, 1957," ed. Richard B. Allen and Nesuhi Ertegun. New Orleans: William Ransom Hogan Jazz Archive, Tulane University.

Goffin, Robert. *La Nouvelle-Orléans Capital Du Jazz*. New York: Éditions De La Maison Française, 1946.

Gottlieb, Robert. *Reading Jazz*. New York: Vintage, 1996.

Gushee, Lawrence. "Would You Believe Ferman Mouton?" *Storyville* 98 (1981).

———. "A Preliminary Chronology of the Early Career of Ferd 'Jelly Roll' Morton." *American Music* 3, no. 4 (1985): 389–412.

———. "When Was Bunk Johnson Born and Why Should We Care?" *The Jazz Archivist: A Newsletter of the William Ransom Hogan Jazz Archive* II, no. 2 (1987): 4–6.

———. *The Story of the Creole Band*. Oxford: Oxford University Press, 2005.

Gussow, Adam. *Seems Like Murder Here: Southern Violence and the Blues Tradition*. Chicago: University of Chicago Press, 2002.

Hair, William Ivy. *Carnival of Fury: Robert Charles and the New Orleans Race Riot of 1900*. Baton Rouge: Louisiana State University Press, 1976.

Handy, W. C. "How I Came to Write the 'Memphis Blues.'" *New York Age*, December 7, 1916.

———. *Blues: An Anthology*. New York: Macmillan, 1926; reprint, 1974.

———. *Father of the Blues*. London: Sedgwick & Jackson, 1941. Reprint, 1961.

Hazeldine, Mike. "Bunk Johnson: The Story So Far." *New Orleans Music* 14, no. 1 (2008): 12–17.

Hazeldine, Mike, and Barry Martyn. *Bunk Johnson: Song of the Wanderer*. New Orleans: Jazzology Press, 2000.

Hazeldine, Mike, and Bill Russell. *Bill Russell's American Music*. New Orleans: Jazzology Press, 1993.

Henry, James Earl. "The Origins of Barbershop Harmony: A Study of Barbershop's Musical Link to Other African American Musics as Evidenced through Recordings and Arrangements of Early Black and White Quartets." Diss., Washington University, 2000.

Herridge, Kevin. "T'was in 'the Cricket' It Must Be So." *New Orleans Music* 9, no. 6 (2001): 13–18.

Hobson, Vic. "Buddy Bolden's Blues." *The Jazz Archivist: A Newsletter of the William Ransom Hogan Jazz Archive* XXI (2008): 1–18.

———. "The Blues and the Uptown Brass Bands of New Orleans." In *Early Twentieth Century Brass Idioms*, ed. Howard T. Weiner, 133–42. Lanham, MD: Scarecrow Press, 2009.

———. "New Orleans Jazz and the Blues." *Jazz Perspectives* 5, no. 1 (2011): 3–30.

Hobson, Vic, and David Sager. "Letters to the Editor." *The Jazz Archivist: A Newsletter of the William Ransom Hogan Jazz Archive* XXIII (2010): 37–39.

Hobson, Wilder. *American Jazz Music*. New York: W. W. Norton, 1939.

Humphrey (the elder), Willie E., and Willie J. Humphrey (the younger). "Interview Digest, March 15, 1959," ed. William Russell and Ralph Collins. New Orleans: William Ransom Hogan Jazz Archive, Tulane University.

Jackson, Preston. "Jazzmen Interviews, Box 16 C." In MSS 559. New Orleans: Williams Research Center, Historic New Orleans Collection.

Jasen, David A., and Trebor Jay Tichenor. *Rags and Ragtime: A Musical History*. New York: Seabury Press, 1978.

Johnson, James Weldon, and J. Rosamond Johnson. *The Books of American Negro Spirituals*. New York: Da Capo, 1925, 1926; reprint, 1969.

Johnson, Joseph French. "The Crisis and Panic of 1907." *Political Science Quarterly* 23, no. 3 (1908): 456–67.

Jones, Louis. "Interview Transcript, Jan 19, 1959," ed. William Russell and Richard B. Allen. New Orleans: William Ransom Hogan Jazz Archive, Tulane University.

Jones, Louis, and Edmund Wise. "Interview Transcript, June 4, 1954, Box 9 B." In MSS 559. New Orleans: Williams Research Center, Historic New Orleans Collection.

Jones, Richard M. "*Jazzmen* Interviews, Box 16 C." In MSS 559. New Orleans: Williams Research Center, Historic New Orleans Collection.

Joseph, John. "Interview Transcript, November 24, 1958," ed. William Russell, Richard B. Allen, and Nesuhi Ertegun. New Orleans: William Ransom Hogan Jazz Archive, Tulane University.

———. "Interview Transcript November 26, 1958." New Orleans: William Ransom Hogan Jazz Archive, Tulane University.

Kennedy, R. Emmet. *Remnants of Noah's Ham (According to Genesis)*. New Orleans: Myers' Printing House, 1910.

———. *The Songs of Aengus*. New Orleans: Myers' Printing House, 1910.

———. *Mellows: A Chronicle of Unknown Singers*. New York: A. and C. Boni, 1925.

Keppard, Louis. "Interview Summary, January 19, 1961," ed. Richard B. Allen, William Russell, and Ralph Collins. New Orleans: William Ransom Hogan Jazz Archive, Tulane University.

Koenig, Karl. *Evolution of Ragtime and Blues to Jazz*. Running Springs, CA: Basin Street Books, undated.

———. *The Plantation Belt: The Musical History of Plaquemines Parish, Louisiana*. Running Springs, CA: Basin Street Books, undated.

———. *The Scrap Book of R. Emmet Kennedy*. Running Springs, CA: Basin Street Books, 2007.

———. *Trinity of Early Jazz Leaders: John Robichaux, "Toots" Johnson, Claiborne Williams*. Running Springs, CA: Basin Street Books, undated.

Krehbiel, Henry Edward. *Afro-American Folksong: A Study in Racial and National Music*. New York and London: G. Schirmer, 1914.

Kubik, Gerhard. "The African Matrix in Jazz Harmonic Practice." *Black Music Research Journal* 25, no. 1 (2005): 167–222.

———. "The Mystery of the Buddy Bolden Photograph." *The Jazz Archivist: A Newsletter of the William Ransom Hogan Jazz Archive* XXII (2009): 4–18.

Laine, "Papa" Jack. "Interview Transcript, April 21, 1951," ed. Edmund Souchon. New Orleans: William Ransom Hogan Jazz Archive, Tulane University.

———. "Interview Transcript, March 26, 1957," ed. William Russell and Richard B. Allen. New Orleans: William Ransom Hogan Jazz Archive, Tulane University.

———. "Interview Digest, February 27, 1959," ed. Johnny Wiggs, Edmond Souchon, Raymond Burke, Jake Scaimbra, William Russell, Richard B. Allen, and Paul R. Crawford. New Orleans: William Ransom Hogan Jazz Archive, Tulane University.

———. "Interview Digest, May 23, 1960," ed. William Russell, Ralph Collins, and Marjorie Zander. New Orleans: William Ransom Hogan Jazz Archive, Tulane University.

———. "Interview Digest, April 25, 1964," ed. Richard B. Allen and Bill Stuckey. New Orleans: William Ransom Hogan Jazz Archive, Tulane University.

LaRocca, Dominick James ("Nick"). "Interview June 2, 1958." New Orleans: William Ransom Hogan Jazz Archive, Tulane University.

———. "Interview June 9, 1959." New Orleans: William Ransom Hogan Jazz Archive.

———. "Interview October 26, 1959." New Orleans: William Ransom Hogan Jazz Archive, Tulane University.

LaRocca, Nick. "Interview May 21, 1958." New Orleans: William Ransom Hogan Jazz Archive, Tulane University.

Lomax, Alan. *Mister Jelly Roll: The Fortunes of Jelly Roll Morton, New Orleans Creole and "Inventor of Jazz."* New York: Duell, Sloan and Pearce, 1950.

Lopez, Ray. "Interview Digest, August 30, 1958," ed. William Russell. New Orleans: William Ransom Hogan Jazz Archive, Tulane University.

Love, Charlie. "Interview Transcript, June 20, 1958." New Orleans: William Ransom Hogan Jazz Archive, Tulane University.

Maggio, Anthony. "The Birth of the Blues." *Overture* 35, no. 9 (1955): 13.

Manetta, Manuel. "Interview Digest March 21, 1957," ed. Nesuhi Ertegun, William Russell, Richard B. Allen, and Robert Campbell. New Orleans: William Ransom Hogan Jazz Archive, Tulane University.

Manetta, Manuel. "Interview Digest, March 28, 1957," ed. William Russell, Robert Campbell, Nesuhi Ertegun, and Richard B. Allen. New Orleans: William Ransom Hogan Jazz Archive, Tulane University.

Marquis, Donald M. "The Bolden-Peyton Legend—a Re-Valuation." *Jazz Journal* 30 (1977): 24–25.

———. *In Search of Buddy Bolden: First Man of Jazz*. Baton Rouge: Louisiana State University Press, 1978; reprint, 2007.

McCullem, Bertha. "Audio Interview," ed. William Russell, Harold Dejan, and Ralph Collins. New Orleans: William Ransom Hogan Jazz Archive, Tulane University.

McCusker, John. "Ory Baptismal Certificate." *Jazz Archivist: A Newsletter of the William Ransom Hogan Jazz Archive* IX, no. 2 (1994): 23–24.

———. "Le Monde Creole: The Early Life of Kid Ory." *Jazz Archivist: A Newsletter of the William Ransom Hogan Jazz Archive* XX (2007).

———. *Creole Trombone: Kid Ory and the Early Years of Jazz*. Jackson: University Press of Mississippi, 2012.

Miller, Ernest Punch. "Interview Digest April 4, 1960," ed. Paul R. Crawford, Richard B. Allen, and Lionel Robinson. New Orleans: William Ransom Hogan Jazz Archive, Tulane University.

Miller, Punch. "Interview Digest, August 20, 1959," ed. Richard B. Allen. New Orleans: William Ransom Hogan Jazz Archive, Tulane University.

Morton, Jelly Roll. "I Created Jazz in 1902, Not W. C. Handy." *Down Beat*, August 1938.

———. "Transcript of the 1938 Library of Congress Recordings of Jelly Roll Morton," ed. John Szwed. Washington: Library of Congress, 2006.

Muir, Peter C. "Before 'Crazy Blues': Commercial Blues in America 1850–1920." Diss., City University of New York, 2004.

———. *Long Lost Blues: Popular Blues in America, 1850–1920*. Chicago: University of Illinois Press, 2010.

Nash, Lemon. "Interview Digest, September 28, 1960," ed. Richard B. Allen and Marjorie T. Zander. New Orleans: William Ransom Hogan Jazz Archive, Tulane University.

"New Sounds from the Crib House." In *Esquire's World of Jazz*. London: Arthur Baker, 1962.

Nicholas, Joseph "Wooden Joe." "Interview Digest, November 12, 1956," ed. William Russell and Charlie DeVore. New Orleans: William Ransom Hogan Jazz Archive, Tulane University.

Odum, Howard. "Folk-Song and Folk-Poetry as Found in the Secular Songs of the Southern Negroes." *Journal of American Folklore* 24, no. 93 (1911): 255–94.

———. "Folk-Song and Folk-Poetry as Found in the Secular Songs of the Southern Negroes (Concluded)." *Journal of American Folklore* 24, no. 94 (1911): 351–96.

Oliver, Paul. "That Certain Feeling: Blues and Jazz . . . In 1890?" *Popular Music* 10, no. 1 (1991): 11–19.

Oliver, Stella. "Interview Digest, April 22, 1959," ed. William Russell and Ralph Collins. New Orleans: William Ransom Hogan Jazz Archive, Tulane University.

Ory, Edward "Kid." "Interview Transcript, April 20, 1957 (for *Life Magazine*)," ed. Nesuhi Ertegun and Robert Campbell. New Orleans: William Ransom Hogan Jazz Archive, Tulane University.

Panassié, Hugues. *Hot Jazz: The Guide to Swing Music*. London, Toronto, Melbourne, and Sydney: Cassell, 1936.

———. *Louis Armstrong*: Da Capo, 1971.

Parker, Willie "Old Man." "Interview Transcript, November 7, 1958," ed. Richard B. Allen. New Orleans: William Ransom Hogan Jazz Archive, Tulane University.

Pavageau, Alcide "Slow Drag." "Interview Transcript, December 10, 1958." New Orleans: William Ransom Hogan Jazz Archive, Tulane University.

Perrow, E. C. "Songs and Rhymes from the South." *Journal of American Folklore* 28, no. 108 (1915): 129–90.

Picou, Alphonse. "Interview Transcript, April 4, 1958, 'Picou' Folder 3.", ed. William Russell, Al Rose, and Ralph Collins. In MSS 536. New Orleans: Williams Research Center, Historic New Orleans Collection.

Picou, Alphonse. "*Jazzmen* Interviews, Box 16 C." In MSS 559. New Orleans: Williams Research Center, Historic New Orleans Collection.

Raeburn, Bruce Boyd. *New Orleans Style and the Writing of American Jazz History*. Ann Arbor: University of Michigan Press, 2009.

Ramsey Jr., Frederic. "Fred Ramsey Speaks Out." *78 Quarterly* VI, no. 4 (1988).

Ramsey, Frederic, and Charles Edward Smith. *Jazzmen*. New York: Harcourt, 1939.

Ramsey Jr., Frederic, and Charles Edward Smith. *Jazzmen*. London: Sedgwick & Jackson, 1939. Reprint, 1958.

Ridgley, William "Baba." "Interview Summary, April 11, 1961," ed. John Handy, Richard B. Allen, and Marjorie T. Zander. New Orleans: William Ransom Hogan Jazz Archive, Tulane University.

Rose, Al, and Edmond Souchon. *New Orleans Jazz: A Family Album*. 3rd ed. Baton Rouge and London: Louisiana State University Press, 1984.

Russell, Bill. "Interview, Feb 2, 1975." New Orleans: William Ransom Hogan Jazz Archive, Tulane University.

Russell, Bill. "Interview, October 1993." New Orleans: William Ransom Hogan Jazz Archive, Tulane University.

Russell, Bill. *New Orleans Style*. New Orleans: Jazzology Press, 1994.

Russell, William. *"Oh, Mister Jelly": A Jelly Roll Morton Scrapbook*. Copenhagen: Jazz Media, 1999.

Rust, Brian. *Jazz Records 1897–1942*. Chigwell, UK: Storyville, 1969; reprint, 1975.

Sampson, Henry T. *Blacks in Blackface: A Source Book on Early Black Musical Shows*. Metuchen, NJ, and London: Scarecrow Press, 1980.

Sargeant, Winthrop. *Jazz: Hot and Hybrid*. New York: Da Capo Paperback, 1938; reprint, 1976.

Schafer, William J., and Johannes Riedel. *The Art of Ragtime: Form and Meaning of an Original Black American Art*. Baton Rouge: Louisiana State University Press, 1973; reprint, 1974.

Schenker, Heinrich. *Free Composition (Der Freie Satz)*. Translated by Ernst Oster. New York: Longman, 1979.

Schuller, Gunther. *Early Jazz: Its Roots and Musical Development*. Oxford: Oxford University Press, 1986.

Shapiro, Nat, and Nat Hentoff. *Hear Me Talkin' to Ya: The Story of Jazz by the Men Who Made It*. London: Penguin, 1955; reprint, 1962.

Smith, Charles Edward. "The Bolden Cylinder." *Saturday Review* December 1957.

Souchon, Edmond. "King Oliver: A Very Personal Memory." *Jazz Review* 3, no. 4 (1960): 6–11.

Spaeth, Sigmund. *Barber Shop Ballads: A Book of Close Harmony*. New York: Simon & Schuster, 1925.

———. *Barber Shop Ballads and How to Sing Them*. New York: Prentice-Hall, 1940.

St. Cyr, Johnny. "Interview Digest, August 27, 1958," ed. William Russell. New Orleans: William Ransom Hogan Jazz Archive, Tulane University.

Stearns, Marshall W. *The Story of Jazz*. London: Sedgwick and Jackson, 1957.

Tallmadge, William H. "Ben Harney: The Middlesborough Years, 1890–93." *American Music* 13, no. 2 (1995): 167–94.

Tichenor, Trebor Jay. *Ragtime Rarities*. New York: Dover, 1975.

Valentine, Kid Thomas. "Interview Digest, March 22, 1957 (for *Life Magazine*)," ed. William Russell and Nesuhi Ertegun. New Orleans: William Ransom Hogan Jazz Archive, Tulane University.

———. "Interview Summary, November 8, 1959." New Orleans: William Ransom Hogan Jazz Archive, Tulane University.

Van Der Merwe, Peter. *Origins of the Popular Style*. Oxford: Clarendon Press, 1989.

Vincent, Clarence "Little Dad." "Interview Digest, December 3, 1959," ed. Richard B. Allen. New Orleans: William Ransom Hogan Jazz Archive, Tulane University.

Vincent, Clarence "Little Dad." "Interview Digest, November 17, 1959," ed. Richard B. Allen and PRC. New Orleans: William Ransom Hogan Jazz Archive, Tulane University.

Weijts, Willem. "Bunk Johnson: Discography." http://www.weijts.scarlet.nl/bjd.htm, 2010.

Whelan, Pete. "Fred Ramsey Speaks Out." *78 Quarterly* 1, no. 4.

White, Amos M. "Interview Digest, August 23, 1958," ed. William Russell. New Orleans: William Ransom Hogan Jazz Archive, Tulane University.

Williams, Alfred. "Interview Summary, April 30, 1960." New Orleans: William Ransom Hogan Jazz Archive, Tulane University.

Williams, Martin. *The Art of Jazz: Ragtime to Be-Bop*. New York: Da Capo, 1981.

Wood, Brian. "Buddy Bolden and Billy the Kid." *New Orleans Music* 9, no. 5 (2001): 6–9.

Wood, Roger. *Texas Zydeco*. Austin: University of Texas Press, 2006.

INDEX

CPSIA information can be obtained at www.ICGtesting.com
Printed in the USA
LVOW08*0818091214

417906LV00005BB/31/P

DATE DUE	RETURNED